OUR NAMIBIA

A Social Studies Textbook
compiled by Henning Melber
within the framework of a project of cooperation between the University of Bremen and the Social and Educational Division/United Nations Institute for Namibia

in consultation with the Department of Education and Culture of the South West African People's Organisation

and financed by terre des hommes (F. R. G.) and the Bremen Senator for Economics and Foreign Trade – State Office for Development Cooperation.

Printed and bound in Great Britain by
Dotesios Printers Limited,
Bradford-on-Avon, Wiltshire

© Namibia Project

First published in the UK by Zed Books Ltd., 57 Caledonian Road, London N1 9BU and 171 First Avenue, Atlantic Highlands, New Jersey 07716, in 1986.
Orignally printed by Terre des hommes (F.R.G.)
Osnabrück 1983/84.

Members of the project-group:

Billy Modise (project-leader)
Social and Educational Division,
U.N. Institute for Namibia, Lusaka/Zambia.

Prof. Dr. Manfred O. Hinz (project-leader)
University of Bremen/Fed. Rep. of Germany.

Nangolo Mbumba (research-fellow)
Department of Education and Culture,
SWAPO of Namibia, Namibia Health and Education Centre, Kwanza Sul/Angola.

Dr. Henning Melber (research-fellow)
University of Kassel/Fed. Rep. of Germany.

Helgard Patemann (research-fellow)
University of Bremen/Fed. Rep. of Germany.

Traugott Schöfthaler (research-fellow)
Max-Planck-Institute for Human Development,
Berlin (West).

Dorothea Litzba (secretarial assistant)
University of Bremen/Fed. Rep. of Germany.

Consultants:

Dr. Mose Tjitendero
Social and Educational Division,
U.N. Institute for Namibia, Lusaka/Zambia.

Shikongo Akwenye
Department of Education and Culture,
SWAPO of Namibia, U.N. Vocational Centre for Namibia, Sumbe/Angola.

Nghidimondjila Shoombe
Representative in the Fed. Rep. of Germany,
SWAPO of Namibia, Bonn/Fed. Rep. of Germany.

Illustrated by Andreas Bund

Proofread by Tim Spence

ACKNOWLEDGEMENTS

This book represents — in spite of many shortcomings — the first systematic attempt in the field of Social Studies to reflect our Namibian past and present within the framework of a new educational system that is helping in the making of an independent Namibia. It is the result of the combined efforts of Namibians of various origin and those who support our ideals for a better future.

We are aware of the many limitations such a first attempt is confronted with. But we hope that it is nevertheless a constructive step towards the realisation of our aims and aspirations for a free and just Namibian society based on human respect, self-reliance and equality.

"OUR NAMIBIA" could never have been completed without the many fellow-Namibians involved in this project. It is meant for them and their aspirations as much as for all those of you working with the material presented. We hope you accept this textbook and find it useful on your own way to a Namibian identity, for which many other things are certainly of more importance than this book. We want to dedicate our efforts to all of you, who by learning contribute towards the better future of our country, turning it really into our Namibia.

Henning Melber

IV

PREFACE

"Our Namibia" is a textbook written especially for teaching social studies to Namibian pupils in upper primary and lower secondary classes. Furthermore, it is the very first Namibian school book and has been compiled essentially by Namibians for Namibians. The "Namibian Project Group" responsible for this book tried to do its best to deal with all aspects of the environment in which Namibian children have to learn today, insofar as this is at all possible under the extreme conditions existing there. The framework of this book resulted from the terrible conditions prevailing in the Namibian Education System (even though the Bantu Education has been formally abolished), and the possibilities offered by the Namibian Education and Health Centres of SWAPO.

Many friends-teachers, church members and politicians-contributed to the success of the book. In particular, we would like to express our thanks to those institutions which enabled the writing of "Our Namibia" through their financial support: the State Office for Development Cooperation at the Senator for Economics and Foreign Trade in Bremen and its head G. Hilliges, and the Organization "terre des hommes" (Help for Children in Distress) of the Federal Republic of Germany and its secretary for African affairs G. Rusch.

It was not by accident that this book resulted from cooperation between the Social and Educational Division of the United Nations Institute for Namibia in Lusaka and the Namibia Project Group of the University of Bremen, Federal Republic of Germany. The long

road of suffering travelled by the people of Namibia is closely connected to the history of Germany and hence that of the Federal Republic of Germany. It was, for example, exactly one hundred years ago that the Bremen merchant Adolf Lüderitz started the process of colonization of Namibia by Germany through his so-called land purchases. After finally breaking the resistance of the Nama under their great leader Hendrik Witbooi, the resistance of the Namibian people was destroyed by German colonization. This was followed by a campaign of extermination resulting in the almost complete destruction of the Herero people. Even today, it is still Germans living in Namibia who influence the future of the country.
This book is, therefore, dedicated to those Namibians who have lost their lives in the struggle against German colonization for a Namibia in peace and freedom.

Lusaka, Bremen, December 1983
Billy Modise   Manfred O. Hinz

VII

VIII

CONTENTS

                                                                  Page

Acknowledgements
Preface

Part I:
OUR COUNTRY NAMIBIA – A POLITICAL GEOGRAPHY

Section 1

Namibia in the world	2
Our Namibian people	3
Namibia – An African country	4
The states of Africa	6
Tears of Africa	9
Africa	10
Our Namibian nation	11
Our country	12
The name of our country: Namibia	14

Section 2

Our community	16
My village	18
A basic physical geography	20
The colonial economy of our country	25
A letter from Kwanza Sul	34
Infrastructure	37
Land usage in Namibia	38
Rainfall in Namibia	40
Land distribution	42

Part II:
OUR NAMIBIAN PAST –
THE HISTORY OF OUR PEOPLE

Section 3
Before the white man came	46
Early nation-building: The peace-treaty of Hoachanas (1858)	48
From the notebook of an early European explorer (1895/1896)	51
The first land theft	54
From the diary of Hendrik Witbooi	57
Good old days	62

Section 4
The German colonial ideology	64
The mentality of white masters	67
Anti-colonial resistance: Chief Kambonde	70
The German-Namibian War:	72
– Samuel Maharero's initiative	73
– The extermination of the Herero nation	74
– The South stands up	78
– Jacob Marengo – Profile of a Namibian leader	81
White opposition to colonial practices	85
Some old people remember their history: King Mandume of Northern Namibia	87
The old Namibian peasant	89
Consequences of defeat: The origins of apartheid	90
The change of masters: South African rule	93

Page

Part III:
OUR NAMIBIAN NATION – SOCIAL EXPERIENCES OF TODAY

Section 5

Evil of the world	96
Forced resettlement:	97
– We won't move!	97
– The old location	99
– The Windhoek massacre	100
– Deportation	102
On contract	104
Life conditions of contract workers	107
Namibian contract worker	111
On strike	112
Resistance and race	118
Unity and self-reliance	120
On colonial mentality	122
Challenging the system	125

Section 6

My mother	128
Leaving home	129
Cecilia Nabot – Profile of a Namibian woman	132
Exile	135
The story of Theresa	136
The strength of women	147
Kassinga	150
Learning for the future:	154
– Our school	156
– Our new school	157
– In the holidays	161
When shall I go	164

Appendix

References	166

Part I:
OUR COUNTRY NAMIBIA – A POLITICAL GEOGRAPHY

Section 1

Namibia in the world

Our Namibian people

Namibia – An African country

The states of Africa

Tears of Africa

Africa

Our Namibian nation

Our country

The name of our country: Namibia

NAMIBIA IN THE WORLD

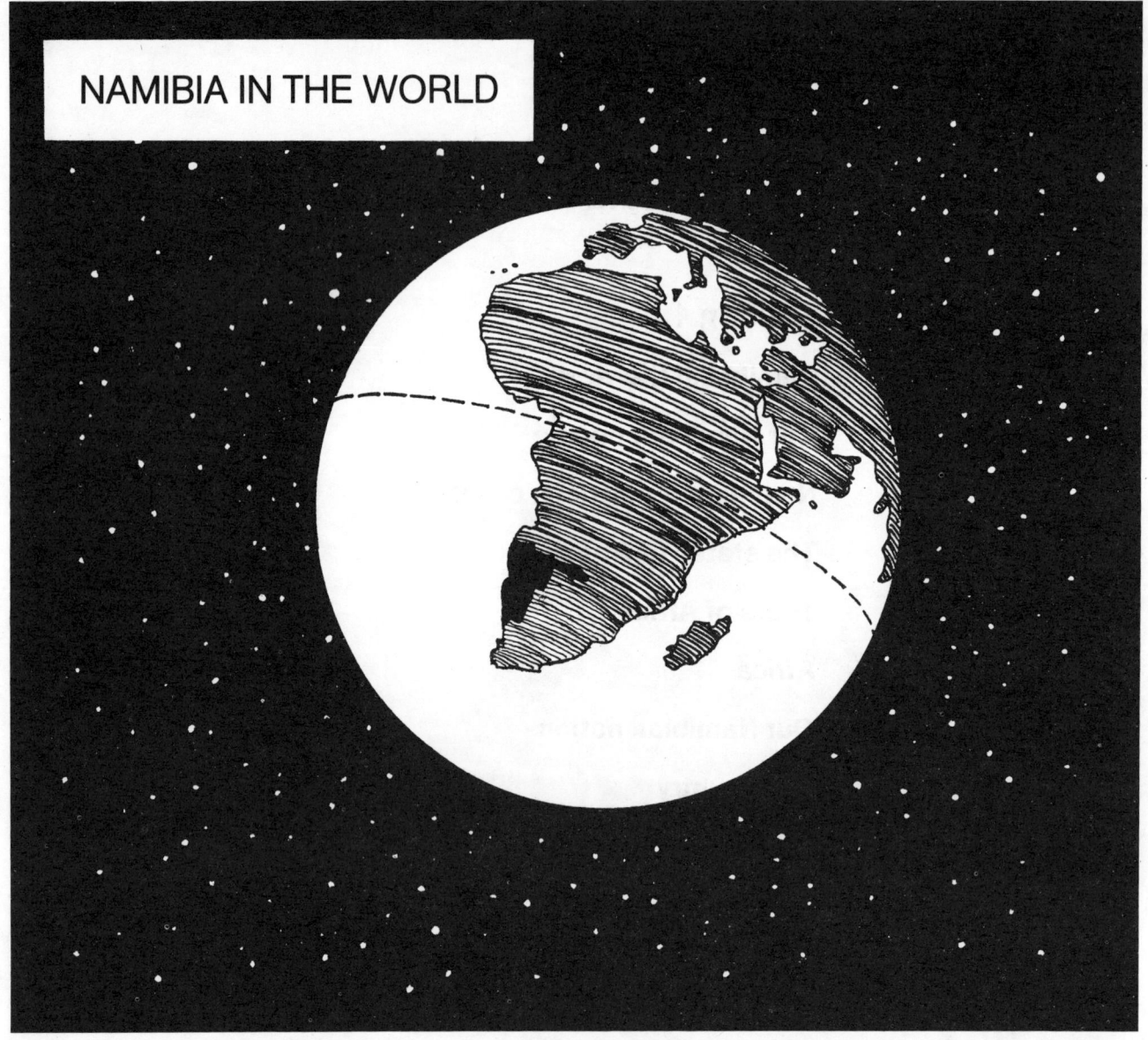

When looking at a globe, you can easily find the African continent, on which our country Namibia is located. Make use of a globe in your school, identify the African continent and our country. For both you can use the above illustration as a guide (note that older globes still call our country "South West Africa"). Look too for the location of the other continents and how they are situated in relation to Africa. Compare their sizes and forms with the African continent and tell each other what you've already heard or know about these other continents, their countries and their people.

OUR NAMIBIAN PEOPLE

There are about one and a half million people who can call themselves Namibians. Most of them are living within Namibia, but a large number is also living outside the country. There are Namibians all over the world, many of them studying at far-away and different places like Western Europe and the socialist European states. Others are in the United States of America. But the majority of those Namibians outside their country are in other African states. Most of them are in Angola and Zambia, as these are neighbouring states that have offered shelter and support to the many Namibian refugees.

This textbook, for example, is used to a large extent in the refugee camps in Angola (places like Kwanza Sul) and Zambia (places like Nyango). Both camps mentioned are Namibian Health and Education Centres, founded and run by SWAPO. These camps and other places for Namibians in exile, like the United Nations Institute for Namibia in Lusaka, the capital of Zambia, are supported by the many friends the Namibian people have in many other countries. We are therefore not alone in the world, but have many people with us.

Tasks:
Those of you who are presently living in one of the refugee camps outside Namibia should be well aware of the fact that many Namibians are abroad. Maybe you have some friends or relatives also outside, some of them even studying at far-away places. If this is the case, then tell your classmates about what you have heard and what you know about these friends and their experiences.

Those of you studying this book within Namibia might have little information about life outside. But maybe some among you in the class have friends and relatives who have gone abroad and have received some information from them. If this should be the case, then pass this information on to the others in your class.

NAMIBIA - AN AFRICAN COUNTRY

Africa is a big continent. With only very few exceptions, nearly all the people of the African continent had been forced to live under European colonial rule. Most of the independent African countries gained independence only during the late 1950s and the early 1960s.

Our country, Namibia, is part of the African continent. It lies in the South Western region of Africa along the coast of the Atlantic Ocean. Her neighbouring countries are Angola in the North, with the Kunene and Kavango rivers serving as a natural boundary. In the South, the Orange river is the natural border to South Africa. In the East, we share parts of the dry Kalahari region with our neighbouring state Botswana.

In 1983, there were altogether 50 independent states on the African continent. They are working together in a common continental organisation called the Organisation for African Unity (OAU). The OAU was founded when the former colonies in Africa became independent, to represent their common interests. The OAU has a Liberation Committee, which supported the struggle for independence in many colonies, where the people were fighting for national unity and sovereignty.

Among the most prominent examples of liberated countries, in which armed struggle had been necessary for winning independence, are some countries in our neighbourhood. In Southern Africa, there are the former Portuguese colonies of Angola, with the MPLA as national liberation movement, and Mozambique, with FRELIMO as representative of the people. Another territory for a long time under foreign rule and white domination is Zimbabwe, which only became independent in 1980, through the leadership of the ZANU/Patriotic Front led by Robert Mugabe.

In our Namibia, the national liberation movement SWAPO is still fighting against the illegal South African occupation. SWAPO in this struggle has the support not only of the majority of the Namibian people, but also of the other independent African states and the United Nations, as well as many other organisations and countries all over the world.

In South Africa, our neighbour to the South, the people are also still fighting against white minority rule, which prevents the black population under the apartheid system from practising their democratic rights as free and equal South African citizens. The most prominent organisation fighting against the unjust regime is the African National Congress (ANC). The ANC was founded as early as 1912 and represents most of the black South Africans, but some Whites are also members of this movement for genuine independence. It has friendly relations with SWAPO, so do most African countries.

Besides we Namibians and the South Africans, there is another people in Africa fighting for its independence. In the North Western region of our continent, the FRENTE POLISARIO is fighting for the self-determination of the Western Sahara.

Tasks:
— *Discuss among yourselves which African countries you have heard about or even know from your own experiences. What organisations do you know, what people from African countries? Exchange your information.*
— *How many independent states are there in Africa?*
— *What is the organisation of African states called and what function do you think it has?*
— *Which countries are not yet liberated?*
— *What prominent movements for the liberation of their countries do you know of?*

Prime Minister Robert Mugabe of Zimbabwe (left), SWAPO President Sam Nujoma (centre), and the Zimbabwean Deputy Prime Minister Muzenda (right) salute the crowd at a rally in President Nujoma's honour in Zimbabwe's capital Harare, June 1981.

THE STATES OF AFRICA

Our African continent has altogether 53 separate states (including the still occupied territories of Western Sahara and our country). You will find them on the map below. Our country Namibia is, with 824,268 square kilometres, among the bigger ones. But with less than 1.5 million inhabitants it is very sparsely populated. Therefore, Namibia ranks among those countries with the lowest average density of population.

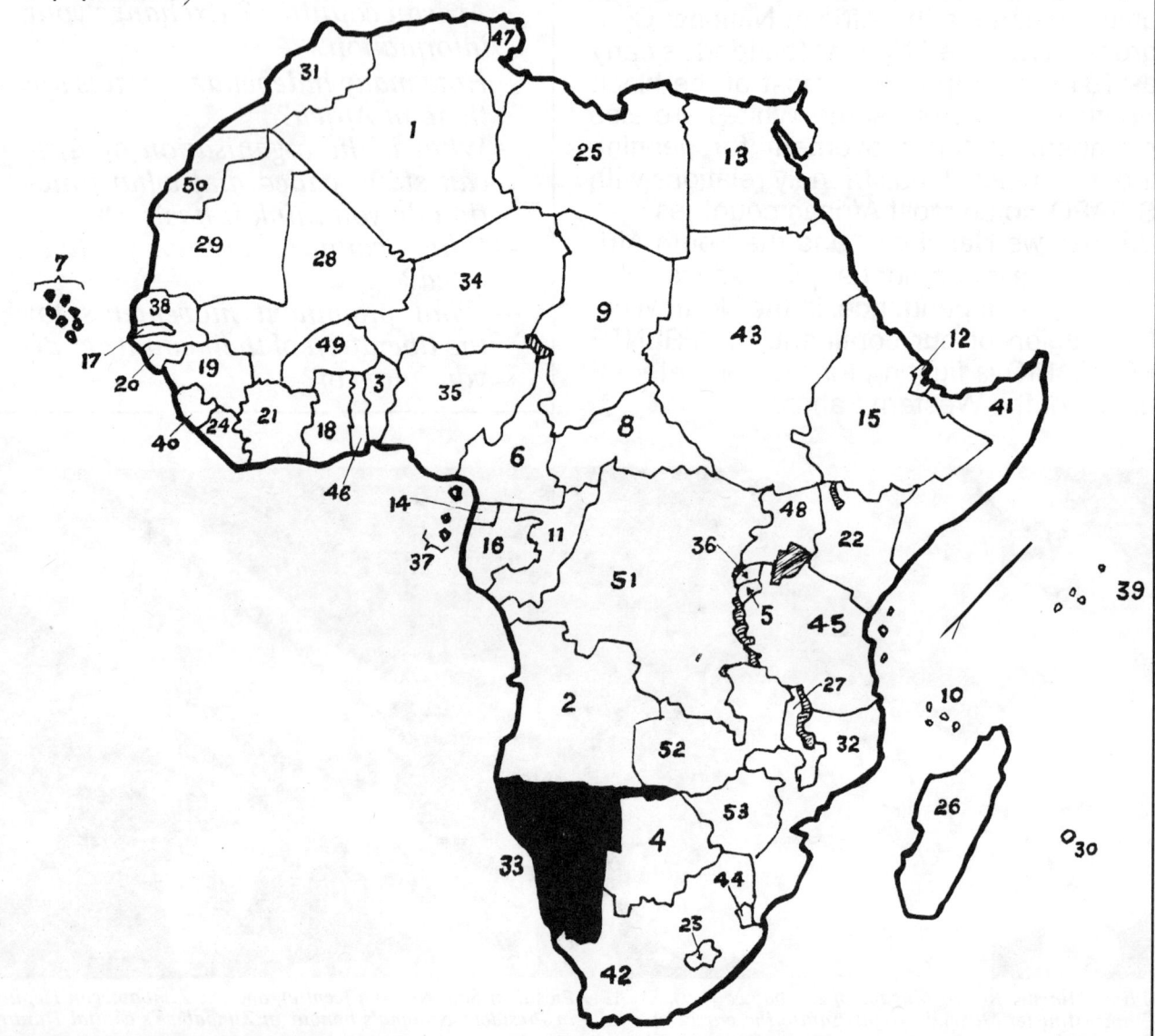

Tasks:
— Look at the size and shape of each of the African countries. Take a globe or map from the school and identify the location of the capitals of these states.
— Follow the alphabetical list with the names of all the African states, their capitals, the size of territory, the population figures and the year of independence, which you will find on the following pages.
— Spot the countries on the map on the previous page by looking for the numbers given to them (they are identical with the numbers of the alphabetical order in the list). Tell each other what you've already heard or know about the different countries and their people.
— Make new lists of the African countries, ranking them under the following headings:
1. area in square kilometres
2. population
3. date of independence.
See where Namibia ranks in each of the lists.
— Find out about the neighbouring countries of each of the African states by using the information of the map and the list. Write down the neighbouring countries of each African state.

Where the year of independence is not mentioned, the territories are either not yet liberated (Namibia, South Africa, Western Sahara) or have not been "classical" colonies with a date of independence from foreign rule (Ethiopia, Liberia). When making a list in the order of the year of independence, put the latter two at the top, the not yet liberated three at the bottom of the list.

THE AFRICAN STATES
(in alphabetical order)

Country	Capital	Size (in square kilometres)	Population figures (1978)	Year of Independence
1. Algeria	Algiers	2.348.895	18.439.000	1962
2. Angola	Luanda	770.161	5.798.000	1975
3. Benin	Cotonou	111.316	3.370.000	1960
4. Botswana	Gaborone	696.320	768.000	1966
5. Burundi	Bujumbura	27.512	3.763.000	1962
6. Cameroon	Yaoundé	469.455	6.770.000	1960
7. Cape Verde Islands	Praia	4.033	270.000	1975
8. Central African Republic	Bangui	609.280	2.250.000	1960
9. Chad	N'Djamena	1.284.000	4.289.000	1960
10. Comoro Islands	Dzaoudzi	2.145	300.000	1975
11. Congo	Brazzaville	355.840	1.448.000	1960

Country	Capital	Size (in square kilometres)	Population figures (1978)	Year of Independence
12. Djibouti	Djibouti	22.000	113.000	1977
13. Egypt	Cairo	989.855	39.745.000	1922
14. Equatorial Guinea	Bata	28.051	326.000	1968
15. Ethiopia	Addis Ababa	1.216.678	30.000.000	
16. Gabon	Libreville	261.760	542.000	1960
17. Gambia	Banjul	10.240	564.000	1965
18. Ghana	Accra	235.116	10.687.000	1957
19. Guinea	Conakry	243.011	4.742.000	1958
20. Guinea-Bissau	Bissau	35.697	482.000	1974
21. Ivory Coast	Abidjan	318.728	5.261.000	1960
22. Kenya	Nairobi	575.898	14.832.000	1963
23. Lesotho	Maseru	29.993	1.109.000	1966
24. Liberia	Monrovia	110.080	1.829.000	
25. Libya	Tripoli	2.073.600	2.240.000	1951
26. Malagasy	Tananarive	588.800	8.000.000	1960
27. Malawi	Lilongwe	116.436	5.448.000	1964
28. Mali	Bamako	1.225.643	6.135.000	1960
29. Mauritania	Nouakchott	1.070.080	1.423.000	1960
30. Mauritius	Port Louis	1.843	940.000	1968
31. Morocco	Rabat	441.344	17.305.000	1956
32. Mozambique	Maputo	762.791	9.949.000	1975
33. Namibia	Windhoek	824.268	1.200.000	
34. Niger	Niamey	1.175.000	4.600.000	1960
35. Nigeria	Lagos	911.360	75.000.000	1960
36. Rwanda	Kigali	26.330	3.896.000	1962
37. São Tomé and Principe	São Tomé	952	84.000	1975
38. Senegal	Dakar	197.120	4.136.000	1960
39. Seychelles	Victoria	278	55.000	1976
40. Sierra Leone	Freetown	70.910	2.578.000	1961
41. Somalia	Mogadiscio	630.156	3.424.000	1960
42. South Africa	Cape Town/Pretoria	1.206.900	26.000.000	
43. Sudan	Khartoum	2.476.000	19.122.000	1956
44. Swaziland	Mbabane	17.165	543.000	1968
45. Tanzania	Dodoma	927.845	16.416.000	1961
46. Togo	Lomé	55.352	2.390.000	1960
47. Tunisia	Tunis	123.700	6.198.000	1956
48. Uganda	Kampala	233.303	11.172.000	1962
49. Upper Volta	Ouagadougou	272.794	6.458.000	1960
50. Western Sahara	El Aiún	284.000	700.000	
51. Zaire	Kinshasa	2.292.091	27.053.000	1960
52. Zambia	Lusaka	743.903	5.381.000	1964
53. Zimbabwe	Harare	384.852	5.900.000	1980

The struggle of the African people for independence from the colonial powers resulted in growing consciousness and awareness of the common situation. Those African states becoming independent supported the continent-wide struggle by founding the Organisation for African Unity. The idea of Pan Africanism influenced many leaders on the African continent.

Tasks:

The common desires of African people are described in the poem following. Read it carefully and find out, what experiences can be identified as general African ones. Discuss especially the following topics:
— colonialism,
— neocolonialism,
— imperialism,
— Pan Africanism.

Find out and discuss, in which way the experiences of the Namibian people fit into the history of African countries, what perspectives are in common and what can be learnt from the history and experiences of African nations.

TEARS OF AFRICA

I
Why the tears Africa?
Your rivers flow with tears!
Your blood is evaporating!
Your flesh – the food of birds!

II
Till when are you going to cry Africa?
Can't you see the red-light?
Can't you hear the whispering
Can't you ever understand–
Understand the language of your children?

III
Mother Africa?
Your children want to fight
Fight and overthrow
The yoke of colonialism, racism and capitalism!

IV
Children of Africa, – Unite!
Whisper no more!
STAND UP AS A NATION,
And fulfil your desires
Desires of Africa

Gerry Wilson Thobias

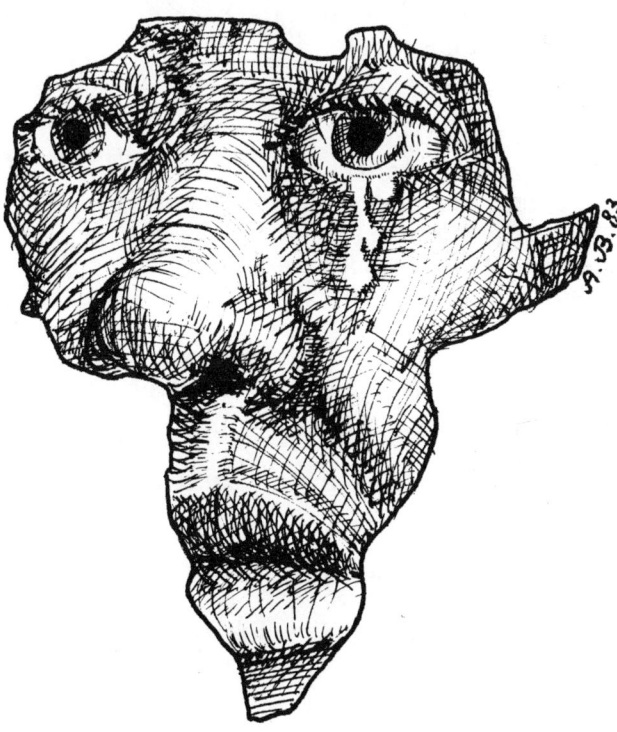

AFRICA

The following poem is taken from a book compiled by a British teacher serving in a Mozambique school shortly after independence. He published his experiences under the title "We're Building the New School". The poem was written by one of his students and deals with the idea of Pan-Africanism. Try to find out what makes this poem Pan-Africanist and what its basic messages are. Further more, discuss what the illustration chosen could mean and why it has been selected for this topic.

AFRICA

Africa my continent
Africa, my continent Africa
Arise, arise
Arise for the liberation
Of all the African people.

Let's fight, let's fight
Fight against the enemy
The enemy that oppresses our friends
The enemy that massacres our children
The enemy that exploits our parents
in the factories, in the mines.

Let's unite ourselves in this great struggle
Let's unite ourselves, let's unite ourselves
Our unity will conquer the enemy
Making Africa
A strong, free, and exemplary continent.

Africa
Exploited and oppressed
Today rises and says
"Freedom, workers of the world!"

Antonio Mussupai

OUR NAMIBIAN NATION

As you can easily see from the previous chapters, our Namibian nation is not only restricted to the Namibian territory. All of our Namibian people are part of this nation. And because many people are living outside the borders of their Namibian home country, the Namibian nation is bigger than Namibia itself.
To be part of the Namibian nation, you have to be Namibian in your identity. This means that all those who come from Namibia or live there, who feel themselves to be Namibians, are part of the Namibian nation. Some people, on the other hand, have been born in Namibia or have lived there for a long time. But by what they do, what they think and how they define themselves, they are not Namibians.

Members of the Namibian nation are all those with a Namibian consciousness. Independent of their age, their sex, their social position, their ethnic or cultural origin. Therefore, the Namibian nation is the result of various different groups of people sharing a common basis of values.

The Namibian nation consists of:
- people of various ages (young and old);
- people of various sexes (girls and boys, women and men);
- people of various origin and race (black and white, different ethnic or tribal descent and those with a mixed cultural background);
- people of various social position or profession (poor and rich, peasants, workers and industrial managers, those with school education and those who have never had a chance to go to school, those with a good job or even a business of their own and the many people without any or with only little income).

These various aspects of a nation (not only typical for our Namibian nation) sometimes create very complicated problems. Therefore, you should discuss the different issues mentioned in more detail.

OUR COUNTRY

Our country's name is Namibia. Namibia is a big country. It has many towns like Tsumeb, Okahandja, Swakopmund, Walvisbay, Otavi and others. The capital city of Namibia is Windhoek. Windhoek is in the central part of Namibia. Namibia lies along the South Western coast of Southern Africa, in the South Western corner of Africa. It has many neighbours like to the North the People's Republic of Angola, to the North East the Republic of Zambia, to the East the Republic of Botswana. To the West lies the Atlantic Ocean. Namibia has three important rivers, namely the Okavango, the Kunene and the Orange river. There are also minerals in Namibia, like Zinc, Diamonds, Salt, Copper, Uranium and so on. Agriculture is also very important, and Fishing. There are four types of transport, namely air transport, road transport, sea transport and rail transport. In Namibia we have many mountains, the biggest mountain is the Brandberg.
I very much like our country.

Felicitas

Tasks:

In her short essay, Felicitas already mentions some basic facts and features of our country. Write down what further characteristics you already know in addition to the information given.

Draw a map of Namibia and mark the places and other geographical features you know about. Compare your knowledge with one of your classmates. You will notice that everybody has the best knowledge about his or her own personal environment. Put together the local knowledge from all of you.

Draw a big map of Namibia on the blackboard or any other suitable place in the classroom and add up all the information you get together collectively and with the help of other people about our country.

Don't be afraid to write down things you are not so sure of. You can always correct mistakes later, and it is much better to make mistakes than to do nothing!

On the next page you find a map of Southern Africa, with Namibia and our neighbouring states. Some of you might have already been in one or more of the other states. Some of you might even be studying this book in an Education Centre in one of these states.

Exchange your knowledge about these states, their relationships towards each other and towards our country. Try to identify the basic features of these countries. Also try to find out the approximate location of the place you are at the moment, when looking at this map.

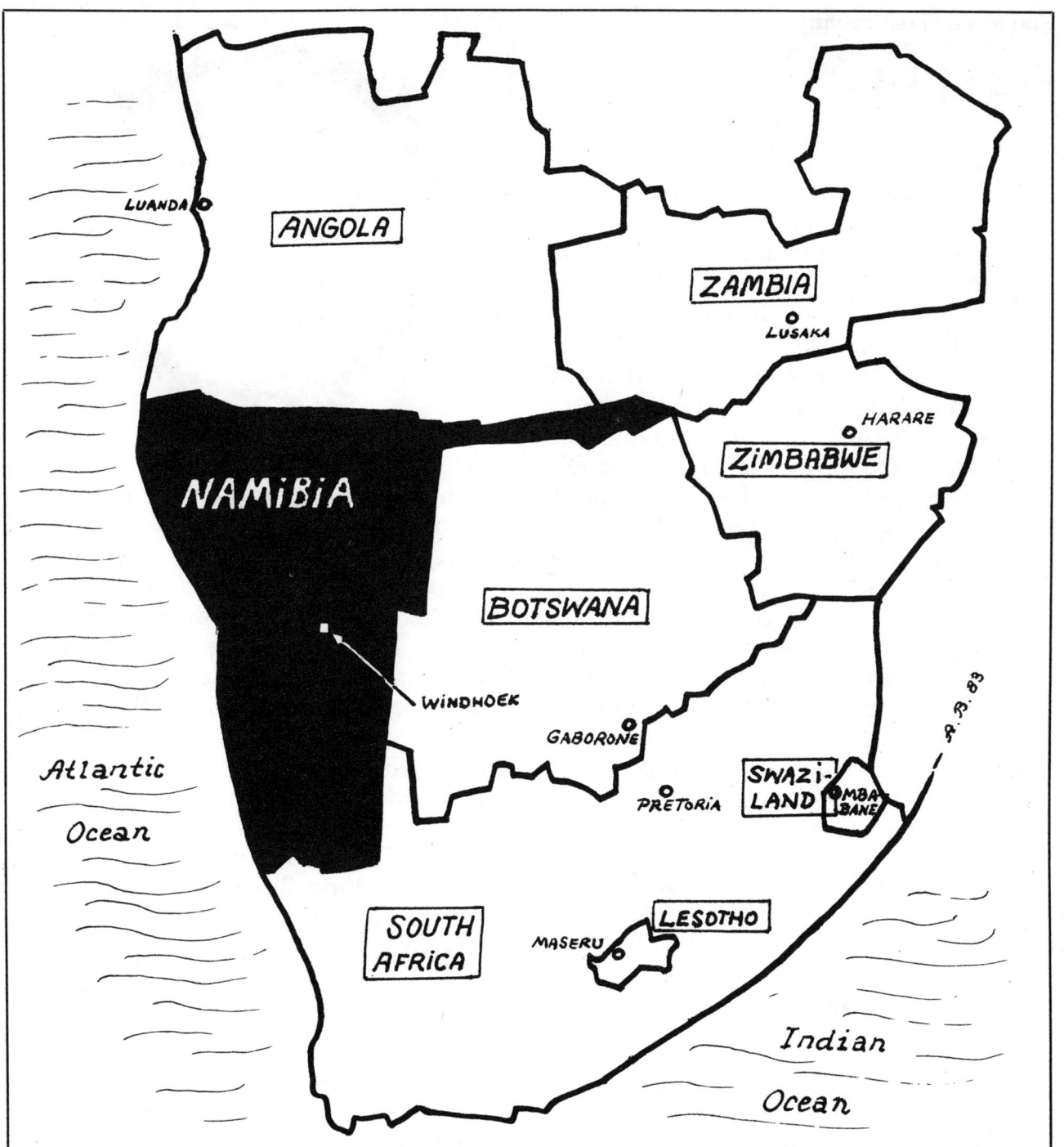

The name of our country:

NAMIBIA

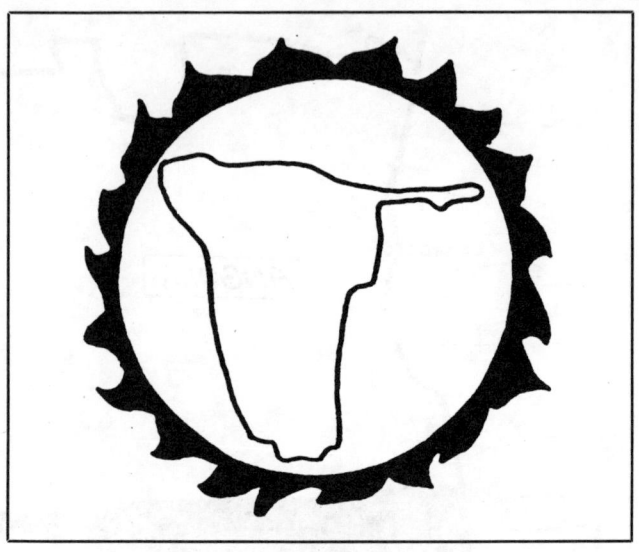

When the Germans came to our country, they colonised the people. In 1884, our country was officially declared a German colony. It was given the name "German South West Africa" by the colonisers. This name indicated where the country lies (on the South Western part of Africa) and to whom it belonged as a colonial object. (— Of course, the land had originally been occupied and used by the African people living there, and it was their possession!) When Germany had to give up her colonies after losing World War I, "German South West Africa" became declared a "mandate", and the administration was handed over to South Africa. The European powers decided on this without consultating the colonised people of our country. From that time onward, our country was called only "South West Africa", as it was not occupied by the Germans any longer.

Finally, in the course of the struggle for independence, our people in SWAPO decided to give their country a name chosen by themselves, NAMIBIA. The choice of this name was based on the following:

For centuries, European traders and explorers had travelled by ship along the African coast. But with the Namib desert as a harsh natural border, the Europeans had for a long time no interest in stopping at the Namibian coast to explore the interior lying behind this desert. It therefore took rather a long time, for the wealth of our country to be discovered by Europeans. These people only came into our territory from the beginning of the 19th century onwards, travelling from South Africa to the North. Consequently, the word Namib, from the Khoisan-language, means shelter. This fact, combined with the wealth of fish and diamonds along the coastal belt, caused our people to re-name the country NAMIBIA.

This name of our country has meanwhile been officially recognised internationally. At the same time, it is an expression of our struggle for independence from any foreign domination, a name of our own given to our country.

Part I:
OUR COUNTRY NAMIBIA – A POLITICAL GEOGRAPHY

Section 2

Our community

My village

A basic physical geography

The colonial economy of our country

A letter from Kwanza Sul

Infrastructure

Land usage in Namibia

Rainfall in Namibia

Land distribution

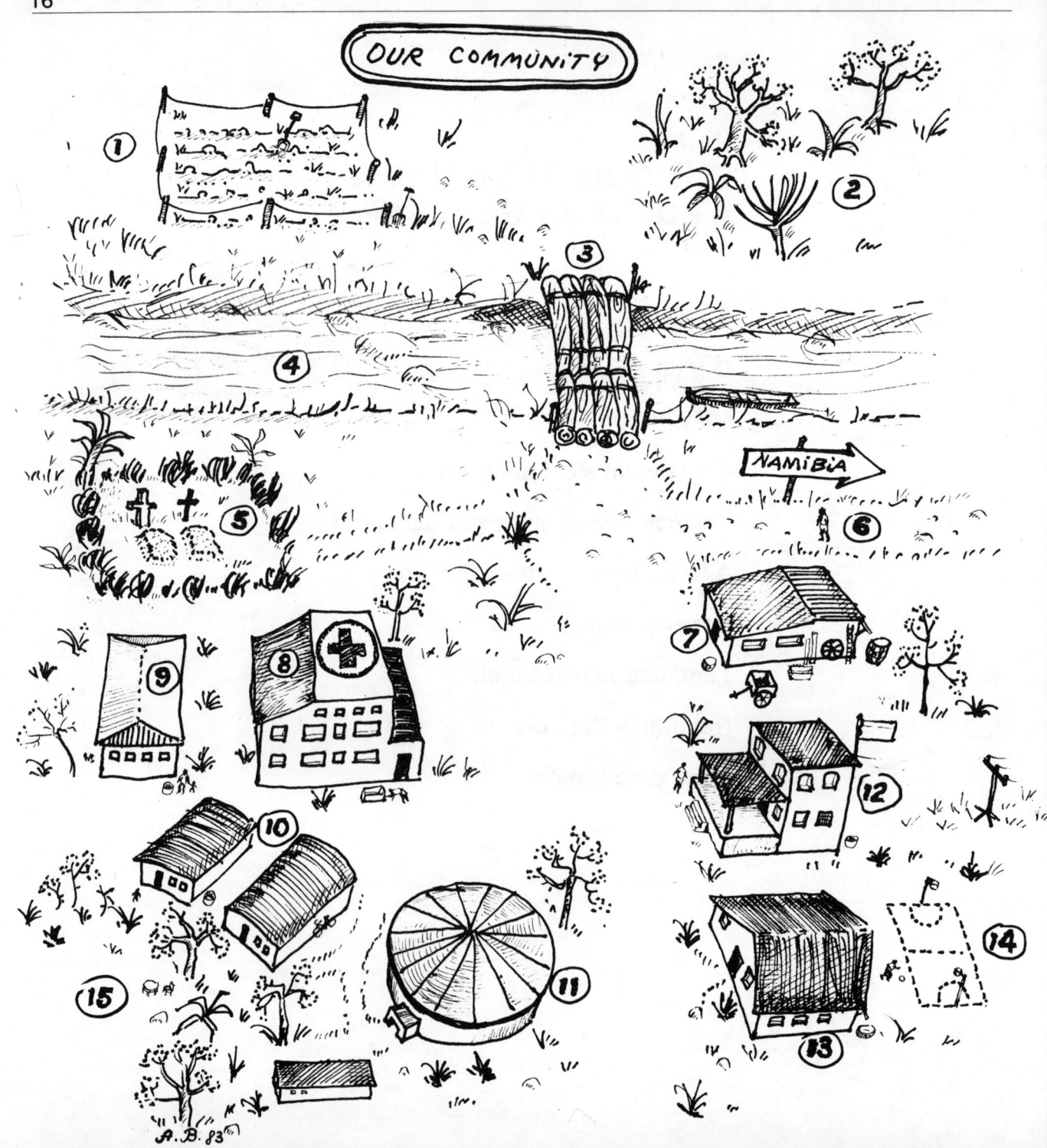

All of us are a part of several different communities. All of them influence our identity. We are all members of the Namibian community living the world over. We are also part of a regional community and a cultural community. And we are part of a village community.

> *List the four various communities mentioned on a wallsheet in your classroom. Discuss each one and finally write down on the wallsheet the characteristics of these communities: a) Namibian community; b) Regional community; c) Cultural community; d) Village or town community.*

When reading this book, you are most likely also a member of another specific community, which has its local centre in the school. It is the community of learners and students (but note, that you can also be a learner all your life and without a school-building!). On this local level, there are several more sub-communities, and you or other people belong to some of them, like the communities of boys and girls, the community of the elder people and so on.

> *Think of the various types of communities existing around you on a local level. List them on another wallsheet in your classroom, discuss each and write down its characteristics (also consider, that within a community like your school further specific sub-communities could exist!).*

Now, we take the camp-village as illustrated on the other page. This picture tries to show some typical spheres of life enclosed in such a community. It wants to illustrate the environment of those living within a refugee-camp in exile.

> *There is one obvious message in this picture, showing that the people are living in a place situated outside our country. Look carefully at this picture and try to identify this clue. Furthermore, tell each other what else you are able to identify.*

Finally, think of the community illustrated as an example of the various possibilities of living together in one way or another. You will find many characteristics, typical for a human community and its organisation in this picture.

> *Make another wallsheet and list the several areas shown in the picture. Discuss and write down details of what you know or can learn about these areas: 1. Field; 2. Wood; 3. Bridge; 4. River; 5. Cemetery; 6. Road; 7. Tools; 8. Hospital; 9. Nursery; 10. Hostel; 11. Church; 12. Administration office; 13. School; 14. Sporting ground; 15. Playground and recreation centre.*

MY VILLAGE

The name of my village is Okaku. It is located in the northern part of Namibia. It is a nice village, and there are many people. These people are very kind, but some are also unkind. There are many animals.

The people of my village are ploughing the gardens, cultivate the crops and also like to hunt animals. For ploughing the fields they make use of donkeys and oxen.

There is a nice building near my village. That is our school, and our church. There is also a shop, where I can buy sweets and skirts. There are some important places where we find minerals. Other places are good for our cattle to get food and water.

I like my village because it is nice and also the people are nice who are living in this village.

Monica

Tasks:
What is the name of your home village? Where is it situated and what does the environment look like? Give a description of your place like Monica does.

Some of you might come from bigger towns. Compare with each other the similarities and differences between towns and villages in Namibia. You will also see that the villages and towns in different parts of our country have different characters. Try to find out what the basic regional differences are and make use of the following list of topics when discussing the subject:
— *climatic conditions (temperature, rainfall);*
— *physical features (landscape around the village);*
— *vegetation (plants growing in Nature);*
— *wildlife (animals living in this natural environment);*
— *economy (what do the people cultivate, breed or manufacture, what techniques do they use?);*
— *infrastructure (what buildings and institutions are there, how is local transport and the supply of water and electricity, how far are the nearest towns and what is offered in the shops?).*

Draw a map of your village or town with those buildings and other features you think are most important. Indicate where your place or house in the village or town is located and where your friends stay.

Draw another map in which you illustrate the region around your village, with the neighbouring villages and/or towns. Also indicate the local natural characteristics (like mountains, valleys, roads, rivers, waterholes, forests and similar features you have for local orientation).

The illustration shows a woman carrying a bucket of water and a baby on her back.

In the background, a man is ploughing the field. What are the typical forms of labour done by people in your village or town?

Make a list and find out whether there are specific tasks carried out by men and women, boys and girls, according to their sex.

Discuss whether this division of labour is necessary and what the reasons for these different responsibilities might be. Consider the possibilities for changing this division of labour. What do you believe could be different in a Namibian village of the future?

Main regional characteristics:

A BASIC PHYSICAL GEOGRAPHY

From the surface (called topography) of our country, we can divide Namibia into three major geographical areas or formations with different climatic conditions, corresponding natural environments and — as a result of this — various typical characteristics with regard to economic activity.

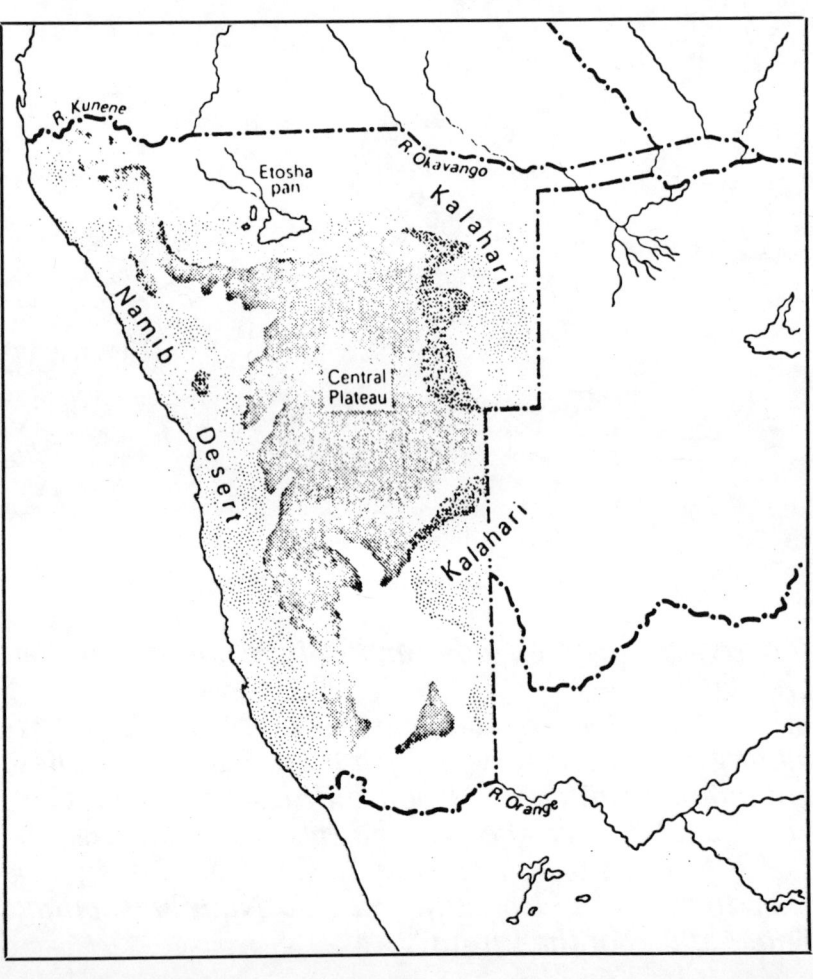

This map roughly indicates the physical structure of our country's surface. — Identify the basic regional features as described in the chapter and compare them with your own impressions and experiences in one or more of the three major areas mentioned. You should be able to give each other many details concerning the natural environment of your home area!

☐ Areas above 1200m (4000ft)
▒ Namib Desert and Kalahari

1) The coastal strip with the Namib desert

This area stretches from the Orange river in the South along the whole coast to the Northern border river of the Kunene. It extends between 80 and 130 kilometres into the country.

The Namib desert is a harsh environment for people, animals and plants. But even there you find life adapted to the difficult conditions. The people have settled along the coast in towns like Oranjemund, Lüderitzbucht, Walvis Bay and Swakopmund. Walvis Bay has the only harbour along our coast which can be used by deep-sea ships. There are smaller ports in Lüderitzbucht and Swakopmund.

These towns and settlements were the result of economic activity. Before the first Europeans had even entered Namibia, people of Khoisan-origin managed to survive at places along the coast, where the towns were later established. They managed to do so mainly by making use of the local vegetation, which they used as their food.

The towns mentioned were built during the early colonial period, some of them for the harbour-facilities they offered, some after the discovery of diamonds earlier this century in the desert belt. Later on fishing on a large scale (starting after World War II, in the late 40s and early 50s) led to the establishment of factories and canneries in Lüderitzbucht and Walvis Bay and caused more people to move there.

The Atlantic coast between Swakopmund and Walvis Bay. At the horizon some Namib dunes.

A view into the so-called "moon valley": Mountains in the Namib desert near Swakopmund.

2) The central part of Namibia with a high plateau

The mountain-slopes of the Khomas-highland stretch from Windhoek westward to the Namib.

The old farm-house at Dordabis, about 70 kilometres south-east of Windhoek, was established under German colonial rule.

The central plateau, or high veld of Namibia covers nearly half of our country's total surface. It has an average height above sea-level of between 1000 and 2000 metres with many mountain slopes. Windhoek, the capital, is situated on the plateau. The climatic conditions there are favourable for people, wildlife and vegetation, although rainfall varies from South to North and leads to different features.

The best grazing land for cattle is situated in the central part of Namibia. This is the reason why the cattle breeders of the Khoisan and Herero people lived in this central area of our country in former times. And this is also the reason why the invading European colonialists had an interest in possessing this area above all, as they were keen to use it for extensive cattle ranching and farming. For that reason, at the turn of this century, the original inhabitants (San, Damara, Khoi-khoi and Herero) were forced by the colonialists to hand over the land they were occupying to white farmers who settled there. To the North of the high plateau, were the settlement areas of the Ambo people. The Ambo had settled there permanently to cultivate the soil. The European invaders did not dare to challenge those people living there and restricted their expansion mainly to the natural border of the Etosha pan, a dry salt-lake, serving nowadays as a big game reserve.

To the South, the average rainfall declines. This area is too dry for cattle to be bred in large numbers. Therefore, mainly goats and sheep are kept on large farms in the possession of white farmers.

3) The Kalahari desert in the East

The Kalahari is the natural border between Namibia and the neighbouring state of Botswana. It has no surface water and is nearly as harsh in its environment as the Namib desert is. Therefore, as Namibia has two deserts in the West and the East of the country, it is sometimes also called the land between two deserts.

> **Note:**
> *Desert encroachment into the land between two deserts is one of the major problems facing independent Namibia. As the extensive farming of the Europeans did not care about the destruction of nature as its basis, cattle and sheep were allowed to graze even in the areas bordering the desert zones in the West and East of Namib and Kalahari. Therefore, desert encroachment started to increase considerably. This means that the government of an independent Namibia has to take measures to stop this process.*

The hostile nature of the Kalahari was used by the German colonial troops in 1904 as a weapon against the Herero: When the Herero resisted German colonial rule, they were defeated in a battle at the Waterberg mountain. After defeat, the German officer in command of the troops ordered them to chase the surviving Herero into the dry Kalahari and to prevent them by military violence from coming back. Consequently, many Herero on their way to Bechuanaland (at that time the name of Botswana) crossed the Kalahari and had to suffer a terrible death from thirst. A few groups managed to escape and reached Botswana.

In the Kalahari desert, only few opportunities for meaningful economic market production exist so far. Mainly sheep and goats are able to live from the scarce soil and the little rain. But one group of our people, the San, have given a good example of how it is possible for people to adapt to local conditions and to develop techniques to survive even in such harsh environment. For a long time, groups of San managed to make a living in remote parts of the Kalahari. They had an excellent knowledge of the local environment, the animals and plants, and knew precisely what to do in order to survive. The San are famous all over the world for this ability. Nowadays, unfortunately, it has become increasingly difficult for these people to continue their traditional way of life, although they had given ample proof that it makes sense. Nevertheless, the San continue to give a striking example of the high culture and ability of indigenous techniques, which allow survival even in basically hostile places like the Kalahari.

Two examples of the famous San rock-paintings:
— A hunting-scene (top)
— A group of people (bottom)

THE COLONIAL ECONOMY OF OUR COUNTRY

A country's economy is a very complicated affair. In this chapter, we are only able to learn about some basic characteristics and features of the Namibian economy, namely those related to what is called capitalist market-production in the three most important economic sectors: mining, fishing and commercial agriculture. These result directly from our colonial past and presently contribute most to our country's economic production and income.

For many of our people, this production offers employment in the mines, factories and on the farms. But the people of Namibia under colonial rule had little or no share in the wealth produced by them and exploited by others. They were mainly employed as unskilled workers with little salary and miserable living conditions. In the mines, the black workers do the hardest labour but get the least pay. Even worse is the income of those employed on the farms. Only a little of their salary is left over to support their families. Under colonialism, the people of Namibia don't get a fair share in the wealth they produce.

In independent Namibia, we have to strengthen our efforts for a fair and just division of labour and income, so that everyone can make a living on his or her own by the work he or she does.

In some cases very sophisticated technology is used by foreign companies for the exploitation of Namibia's raw materials. The photo below shows machinery used at the diamond fields in the Namib desert along the coast.

Mining

Among the natural wealth of our country, mineral raw materials are those which contribute the most to the economic income. The minerals exploited by large foreign companies in possession of foreigners are sold abroad, and little of this wealth benefits the Namibian people.

The new administrative centre of Consolidated Diamond Mines under construction in Windhoek.

Large diamond fields along the coast and in the Namib desert were discovered early this century and since then have contributed most to the income from mining. Until now, the profit has served foreign mining companies. In the case of diamonds, it is the Consolidated Diamond Mines from South Africa which has the benefit of large profits every year.

Another important raw material is the uranium oxide, so-called "yellow cake", exploited at the Roessing mine some forty kilometres inland from Swakopmund. It is mainly owned by the British Rio Tinto Zinc mining company, but some other mining companies from various countries also have a share in this operation and the profit that is made.

Other important mines are situated in the area of Tsumeb, Namibia's second largest town, which is basically a mining centre for exploitation of the rich copper deposits. The biggest enterprise there is the American Tsumeb Corporation, which produces large quantities of copper ore for sale abroad.

Together, there are about twenty important mining operations in Namibia, which exploit a lot of various metals and minerals of international importance. They are all run by foreign companies. These companies sell the produced raw material abroad and keep the profit for themselves. Much of this money never comes back to Namibia to be used there, but is kept instead in the home countries of these companies.

The Roessing uranium mine is one of the largest open-cast uranium mines in the world.

Above: Headgear at a shaft of the Tsumeb copper mine, the deepest in Namibia.

Right: Miners waiting for transport into one of the deep shafts to work far below the surface under hard conditions.

Red-hot copper is poured into forms at a smelter.

Part of the copper mine at Tsumeb.

This map indicates to you the places and names of the biggest mining enterprises within our country.
— If you know anybody who has been employed as a miner there, try to obtain a description of the place and the work done there.

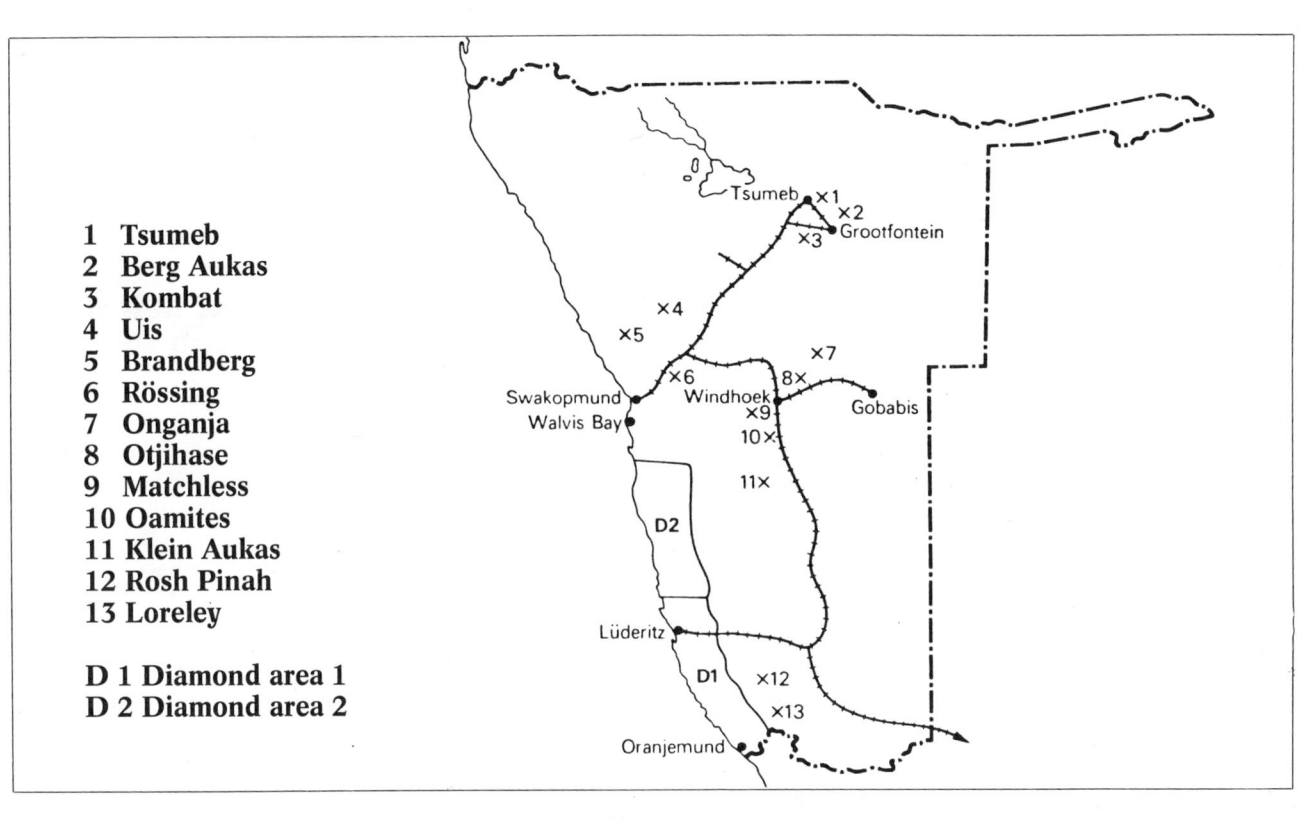

1 **Tsumeb**
2 **Berg Aukas**
3 **Kombat**
4 **Uis**
5 **Brandberg**
6 **Rössing**
7 **Onganja**
8 **Otjihase**
9 **Matchless**
10 **Oamites**
11 **Klein Aukas**
12 **Rosh Pinah**
13 **Loreley**

D 1 Diamond area 1
D 2 Diamond area 2

Beach mining at the coast.

Workers at the diamond fields near Oranjemund.

Fishing

At the Atlantic coast, fish used to live in huge quantities and variety of species. The Namibian coast had once been one of the richest regions for fish in the whole of Africa. South African companies built some fishing industry (factories and canneries) in Walfish Bay and — to a lesser extent — Lüderitzbucht in the early 1950s and sent large numbers of fishing trawlers to sea to catch as much fish as possible. Meanwhile, the stock of fish has nearly been destroyed, and the factories are out of operation most of the time because of lack of fish.

This is a prominent example of the destruction of natural wealth and natural balance. Plenty of fish could have been caught and processed in the factories, where they are put into tins. But it would have been important to leave enough fish to enable replenishment of stocks. By means of careful fishing we would now still have an important economic income and plenty of food from the sea. But the economic interest of the factory-owners meant them gaining as much profit in as short a time as possible. And now we are robbed of this natural wealth that once existed.

Fish being pumped from a trawler at Walfish Bay. Due to over-exploitation, the fishery reserves have been depleted and catches have declined in recent years.

An independent Namibian government will have to pay a great deal of attention to this problem. One of the major tasks has to be to initiate a careful farming of the small stock of fish left, so that it may one day recover and allow regular fishing again on a basis ensuring that this resource is not exhausted again. We can then continue to make use of this natural wealth, but we have to be careful not to destroy it once more.

As in the case of the problem of desert encroachment mentioned above, we have to learn from the experiences of the past to avoid mistakes in the future.

The two photos show completely different ways of catching fish: On top, fishermen on a trawler exploit the wealth of the sea. On the left, the local people in the northern border areas catch fish in the rivers and swamps for personal consumption.

Commercial agriculture

Mainly large farms in the possession of white farmers contribute to a considerable extent to the export of Namibian products. Cattle-ranching for market-production (i. e. breeding cattle to sell the beef afterwards) is carried out by farmers on the central plateau up to the Etosha pan, as rainfall is sufficient for big livestock. In former times, tremendously big herds of cattle grazed in this region. They were owned by the Herero and — to a lesser degree — by groups of Khoisan people. Nowadays, only the white farmers have such huge herds of cattle. In early times, they took the land and cattle from the Africans living there. The cattle are nowadays either slaughtered in Namibia itself in abbatoirs situated in larger towns like Okahandja and Omaruru, or directly loaded onto trains and sent to South Africa, to be sold on the cattle-markets there. Cattle farming is one of the two main sources of income in the field of commercial agriculture.

A meat processing factory.

Above: A day-old Karakul lamb.
Below: One of the expensive fur coats.

The other main source of income in agriculture by European farmers is Karakul breeding. Karakul sheep were brought to Namibia early this century by German farmers, who realised that the dry climate in the southern parts of our country were favourable for breeding sheep (the Khoisan people originally living there already kept various sorts of sheep and goats). The lambs of the Karakul sheep are slaughtered, their fleeces then sold as those of Persian lambs. These are used mainly in Europe and North America for manufacturing expensive coats and jackets for women. The Karakul industry is one of the economic activities that has contributed greatly to the wealth of white farmers. The fleeces are exported as raw material and sold in international auctions for further processing.

Our country's economic structure is shown and explained below. But a very important economic activity, called subsistence production, is not expressed in this map. Subsistence production means that the people produce on the land and in the household just what they need for their personal life (mainly food production for their own consumption) or could sell on the local market. It is the economic activity which, by number, occupies most Namibians in the reservations, as there are no other means for survival and no employment opportunities to give cash income.

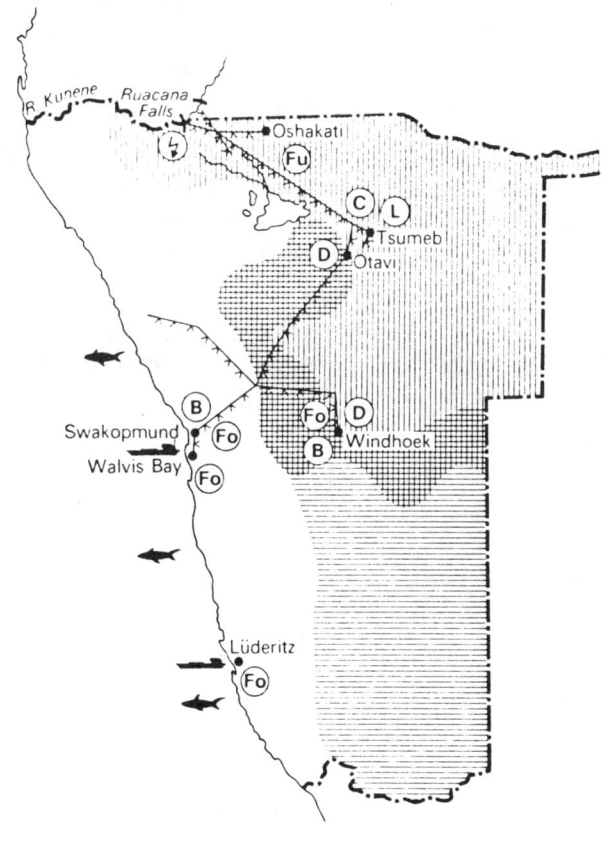

Fo food industry
Fu furniture factory
C copper smelter
L lead smelter
D dairy production
B breweries

fishing
power station
harbour
power line
cattle
sheep and goats

Tasks:
What do you think justifies characterising our country's present economic structure as a colonial one? — Give reasons for your opinion!
What should be changed after independence?
What other sectors of an economy do you know of besides those mentioned in this chapter?
List the kind of employment of people you know: where they work, what they do? What other economic activities exist besides those in the sectors mentioned?
Where do you think do the priorities for an independent economic development lie?

A LETTER FROM KWANZA SUL

> Namibia Education Centre
> Kwanza Sul
> People's Republic of Angola
> 7th September, 1982.
>
> Dear Kamkoto,
> my main aim in writing this letter to you is to tell you about our school here. Our school is called the Namibian Education Centre. It is a big school with many teachers and students. It is located in the south of Kwanza Province in the People's Republic of Angola. Our school is near a very big plantation. They cultivate coffee plants on this plantation. The Angolans sell this coffee and they can get some money from other countries for this.
> We have books, pens, pencils, tables, chairs, benches and other materials for teaching and learning in our school. We have to learn many subjects, and sometimes it is difficult, but we try to do our best.
> Pass on my regards to all friends,
> your best friend
>
> Elisabeth

You also have to learn a lot, and you use this book to help.
Sometimes you might also find it difficult, but certainly you are also trying your best.

Besides the information on the school, this letter deals with another important subject, which is the theme of this paragraph. In her letter, Elisabeth refers to the coffee-plantation near the camp. She mentions that the cultivation of coffee by the Angolans is done to sell this coffee afterwards.

This is something very usual: some countries have a climate and conditions suitable for the cultivation of special products like coffee, tea, cocoa or other agricultural foodstuff. They produce more than they actually need for themselves. This is then sold to others abroad to get foreign money. We call this export. With the money, these countries can buy other things they need, which they don't produce themselves. We call this import. The export-oriented production of raw material like agricultural products or mineral resources sometimes results in what is called mono-cultures. This means that the people produce above all for sale on the world market.

In Namibia, we are not able at present to produce agricultural crops for export, but we have enough cattle not only to supply our local needs, but also to sell beef on foreign markets. With karakul sheep, we produce the fleece of the Persian lambs almost exclusively for export. And mineral resources like uranium, diamonds, copper and zinc have long been exploited by mining companies to be used for production in other industrial countries.

The illustration shows the production circle for coffee. Look at the various pictures and discuss with each other which stages of production, and finally consumption, are shown.
Think about other products you know of which demonstrate a similar process. Try to scetch another such circle with one of the raw materials produced in our Namibian country.

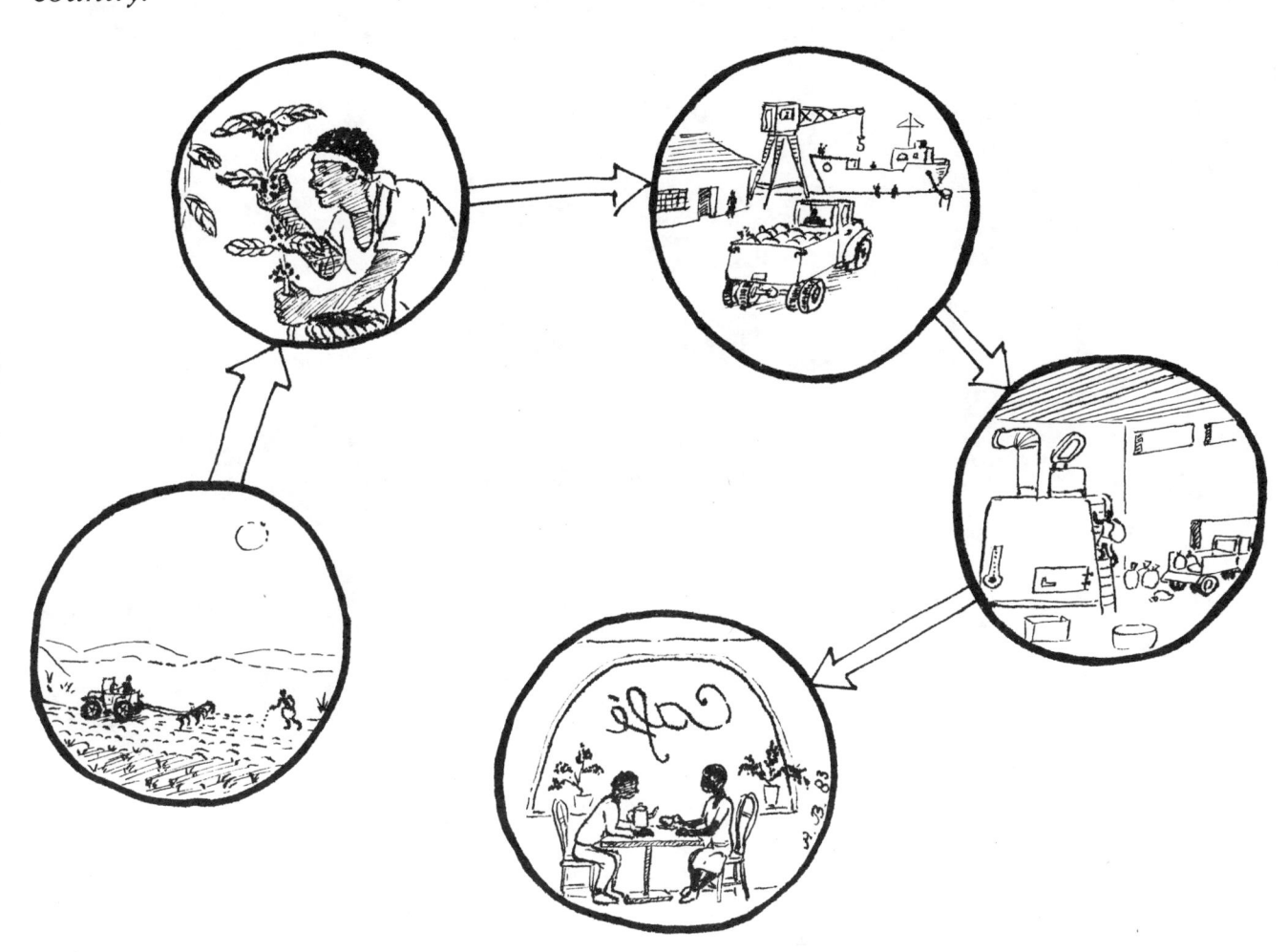

Make a list of what is produced in our country for export and discuss for what purpose this raw material is needed elsewhere. Make another list of items that you believe are needed in our country and have to be imported. Consider whether the items are really needed, i.e. if they are basic commodities for our people. Discuss each item in the class before you finally decide.

Coffee (above a photo from Kenya showing beans being dried in the sun) is a very common export commodity from African and Latin American countries. — Do you know any others?
We in Namibia produce no coffee ourselves, as the climatic conditions that exist are not very favourable. But of course, we have other products to offer for sale abroad. — Do you know some of them?

Karakul pelts are marketed internationally under the trade-mark SWAKARA and contribute considerably to Namibia's foreign income. The photo above shows the manufacturing of furs. Diamonds play a vital role in the economy and gemstones are also found in large numbers, although they are of minor importance for economic exports. But there are a lot of skillful jewellers (photo below).

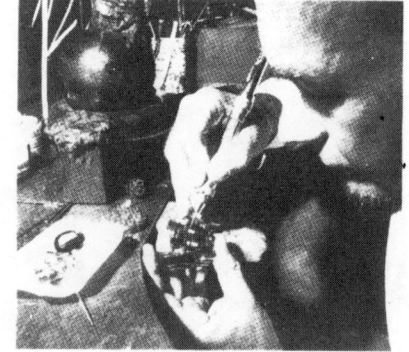

These photos show some typical features of large-scale, mechanised, commercial agricultural production for so-called cash-crops: An irrigation-scheme (left) and the use of chemical fertilizers and/or pesticides (picture right) to improve the output of the crops for sale on the (world)-market. Both scenes are from the northern parts of Namibia, where such production already takes place to a limited extent.
— Compare these methods with those of soil-cultivation you know from personal experience! What are the differences?

INFRASTRUCTURE

With the word infrastructure we refer to those features of a region or country related to the problems of transport and communication. These are sometimes natural phenomena like lakes, rivers, mountains and other features influencing the construction of a transport and communication network. In the case of our country Namibia, there are mainly the deserts as natural borders for an infrastructure, as of course very few people are living in the Namib and the Kalahari areas.

— *Look at the map below and identify those features marked as infrastructure. Discuss their importance.*

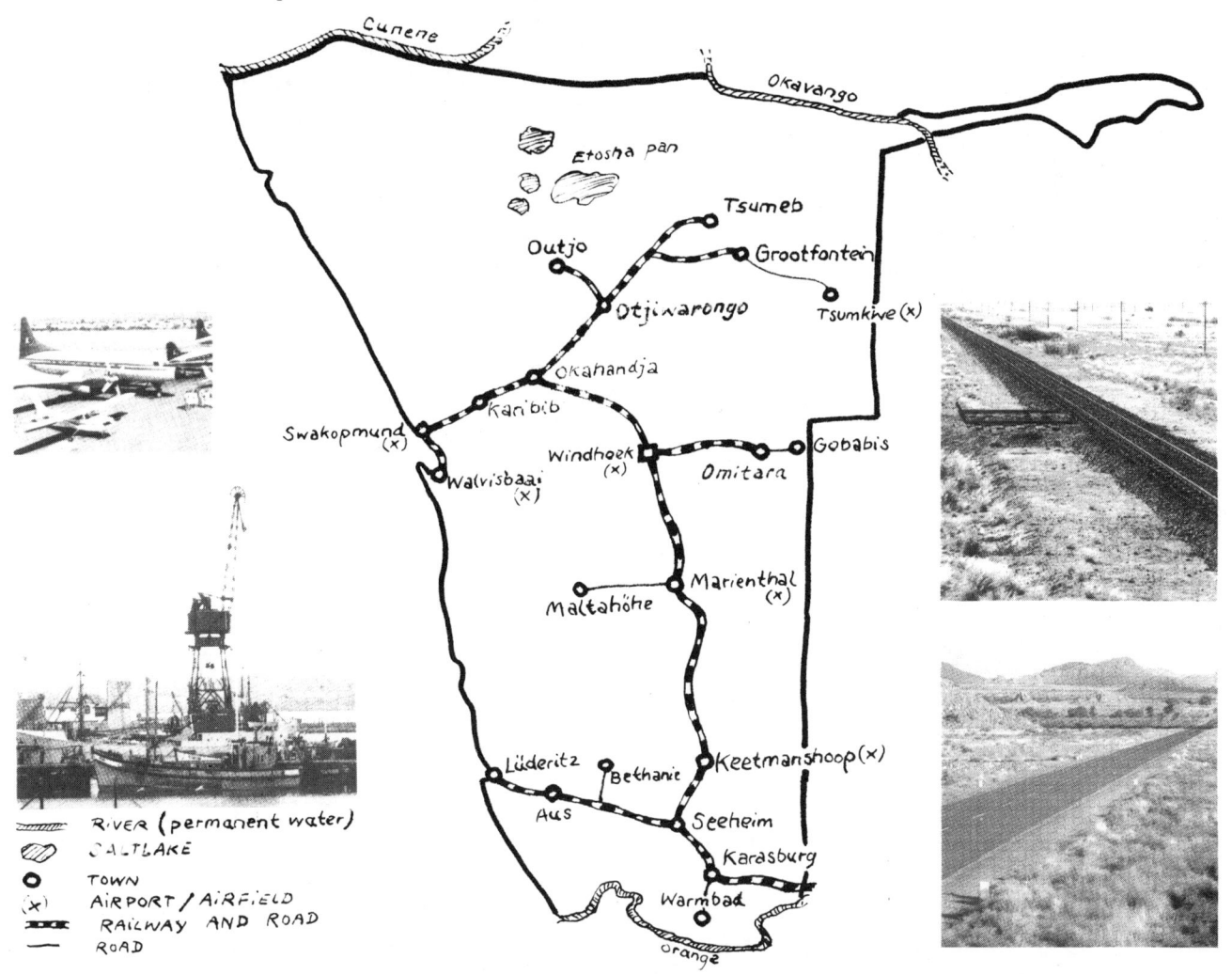

Legend:
- RIVER (permanent water)
- SALTLAKE
- ○ TOWN
- (X) AIRPORT / AIRFIELD
- RAILWAY AND ROAD
- ROAD

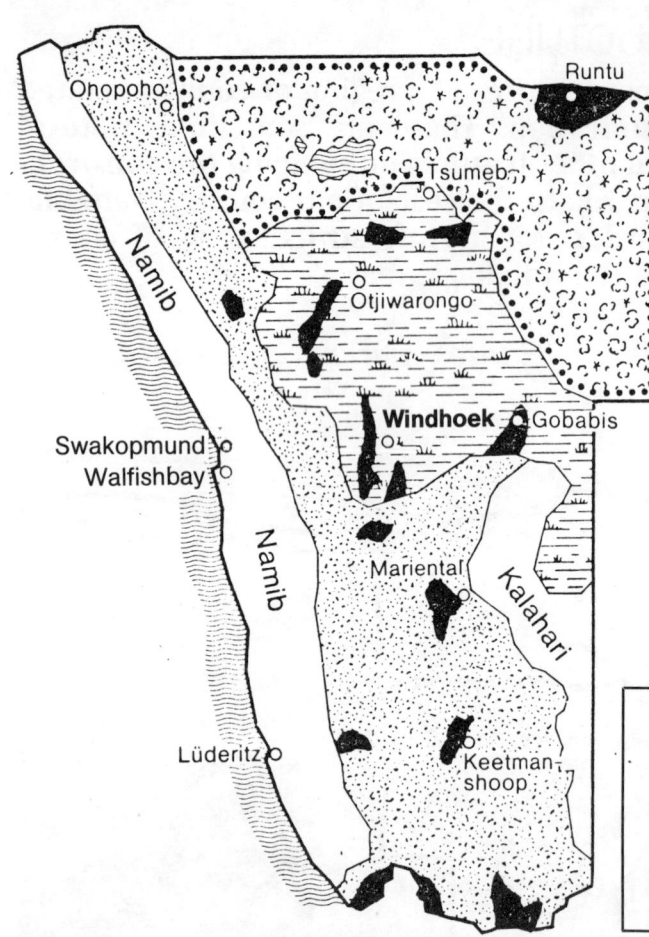

LAND USAGE IN NAMIBIA

This map shows you how the various regions of our country are used and cultivated according to existing climatic and geographical conditions.
— Only about 1.1 per cent of Namibia's whole area is suitable for intensive soil cultivation!

Those of you coming from various regions of our country, should explain to the others the characteristics of the environment at home and the dominant agricultural production typical for the area.

- **Desert**
- **Semi-desert, scarce vegetation with goats and sheep breeding**
- **Dry savanna (grass and thorn shrubs) with cattle breeding**
- **Dry savanna (grass and trees) with dryland cultivation and smallstock**
- **Dry forest belt**
- **Soil cultivation and intensive stock breeding with irrigation**

The map illustrates the various ecological zones and their potential for agricultural production.

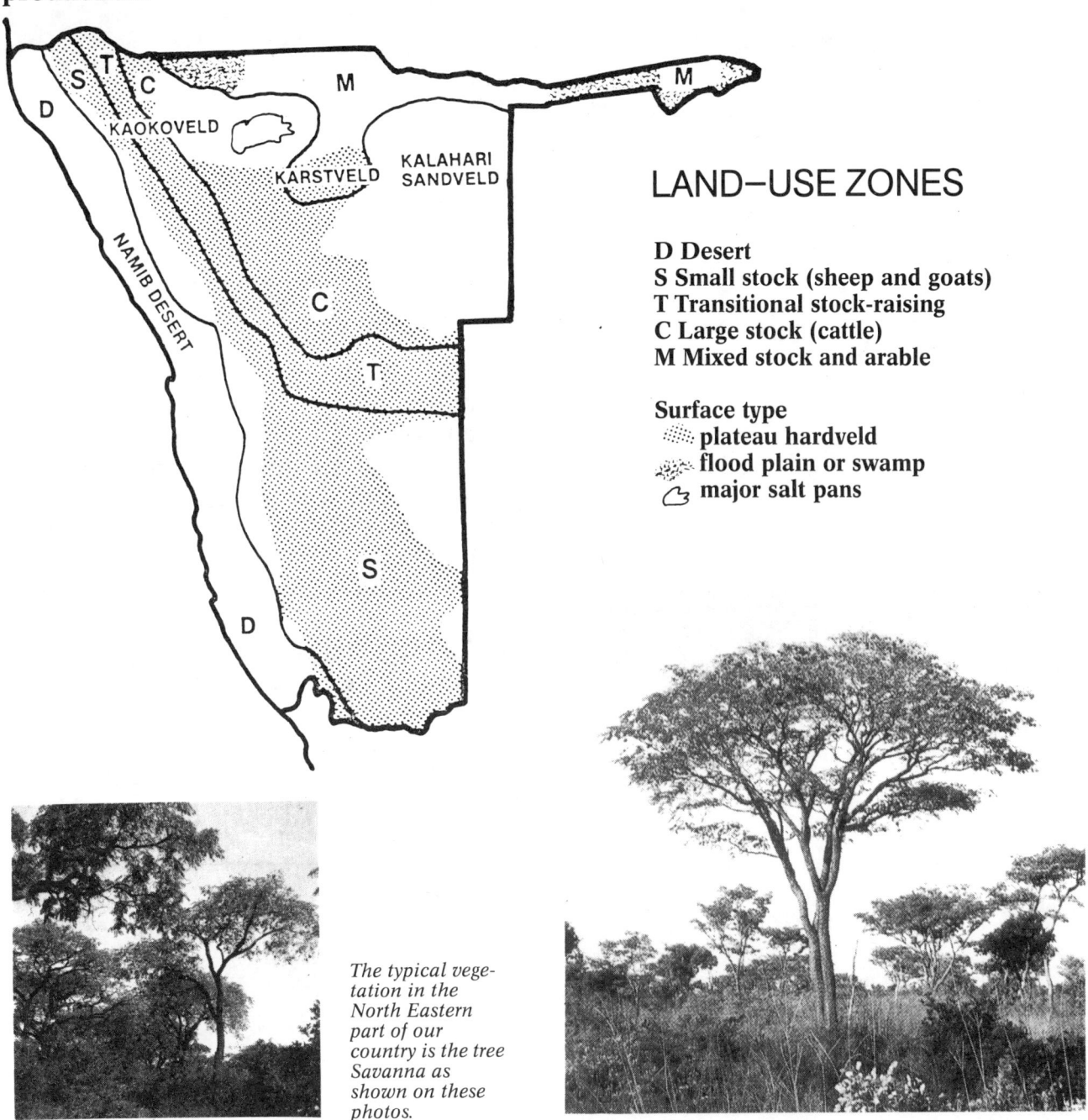

LAND–USE ZONES

D Desert
S Small stock (sheep and goats)
T Transitional stock-raising
C Large stock (cattle)
M Mixed stock and arable

Surface type
plateau hardveld
flood plain or swamp
major salt pans

The typical vegetation in the North Eastern part of our country is the tree Savanna as shown on these photos.

RAINFALL IN NAMIBIA

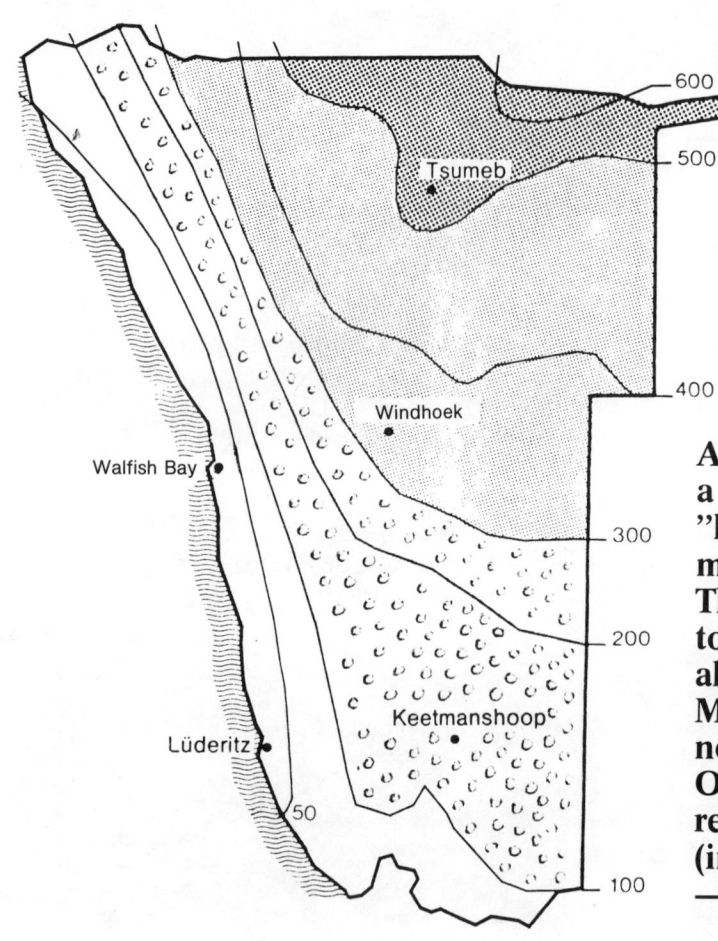

Map showing average annual rainfall across Namibia, with labeled locations: Tsumeb, Windhoek, Walfish Bay, Lüderitz, Keetmanshoop. Isohyets shown at 50, 100, 200, 300, 400, 500, and 600 mm.

Average annual rainfall

- Below 100 mm
- 100 to 300 mm
- 300 to 500 mm
- above 500 mm

As you all know, we live in or come from a very dry country (sometimes called the "land between two deserts") which is very much dependent on the annual rainfall. This rainfall differs in average from region to region, with the least amount of rain along the coast and in the southern parts. Most rain falls, in normal years, in the northern parts of Namibia.

On the map you can see the approximate regions and the average amount of rainfall (in mm) over one year.

— About 70 per cent of our country's surface has a poor annual rainfall!

Compare this map with the one on land usage in our country. Can you explain why water is so necessary and why we have only such a small proportion of land (1.1 per cent) in our country suitable for intensive soil cultivation?

Discuss the problem of droughts and what you think could be done to reduce the risks and consequences of such a natural catastrophe with regard to hunger and water supply.

During the rainy season we sometimes have plenty of water!

LAND DISTRIBUTION

1) The settlement patterns before colonisation

In our country, the land issue has long been of central importance to the Namibian people. During the days before European colonialism influenced our history and development, the cattle-breeding communities in the southern and central part of our country tried to have as much influence as possible over as large parts of land as were necessary for their needs in grazing the cattle.

In times of ecological constraints, especially droughts, the competition for land increased mainly between the Nama communities and the Herero groups. The first Europeans coming to Namibia tried to make use of these disputes to help pave the way for a colonial system. The map on this page indicates the approximate main areas of settlement within the borders of our country before colonization. It shows that Namibia had few areas remaining outside any meaningful control or influence by one of the communities at that time.

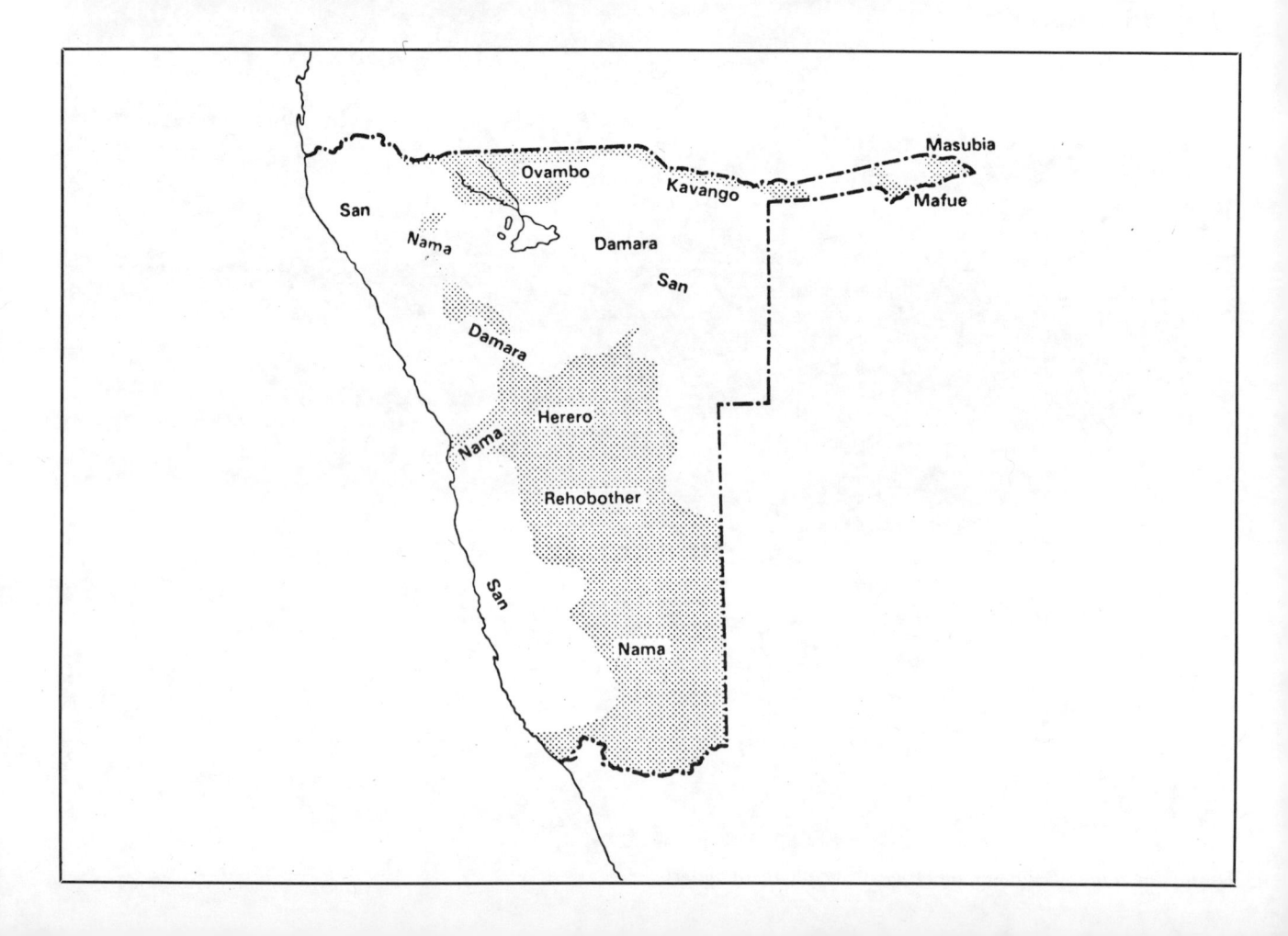

2) The creation of 'reserves' for the African population

German colonialism not only tried to gain influence by making use of sectional interests and rivalries concerning the land question. After having established control over Namibia, the German colonial authorities went further by introducing as early as the end of the 19th century, reserves for the various Namibian communities. After the final defeat of Herero and Nama in the course of the German-Namibian War (1904-1907), the colonial administration developed a systematic policy of separation and control of the Namibian population by creating reserves for each of the communities. At the end of the German colonial period, more than 20 such areas existed, in which the Namibians, depending on their tribal origin, were forced to stay. The main areas of useful land in the central and southern parts of Namibia were either occupied by white farmers or in the possession of land companies. The map on this page indicates the reserves created under German colonialism and existing until the early 1960s.

To the north, the Germans introduced a border line dividing the settlement areas of the Ovambo and other communities living there from the rest of Namibia, which then was called the 'Police Zone'. The reason for this had been that direct control and influence over the people was maintained only within this 'Police Zone', while the people living in the northern settlement areas were only indirectly incorporated into the German colonial system.

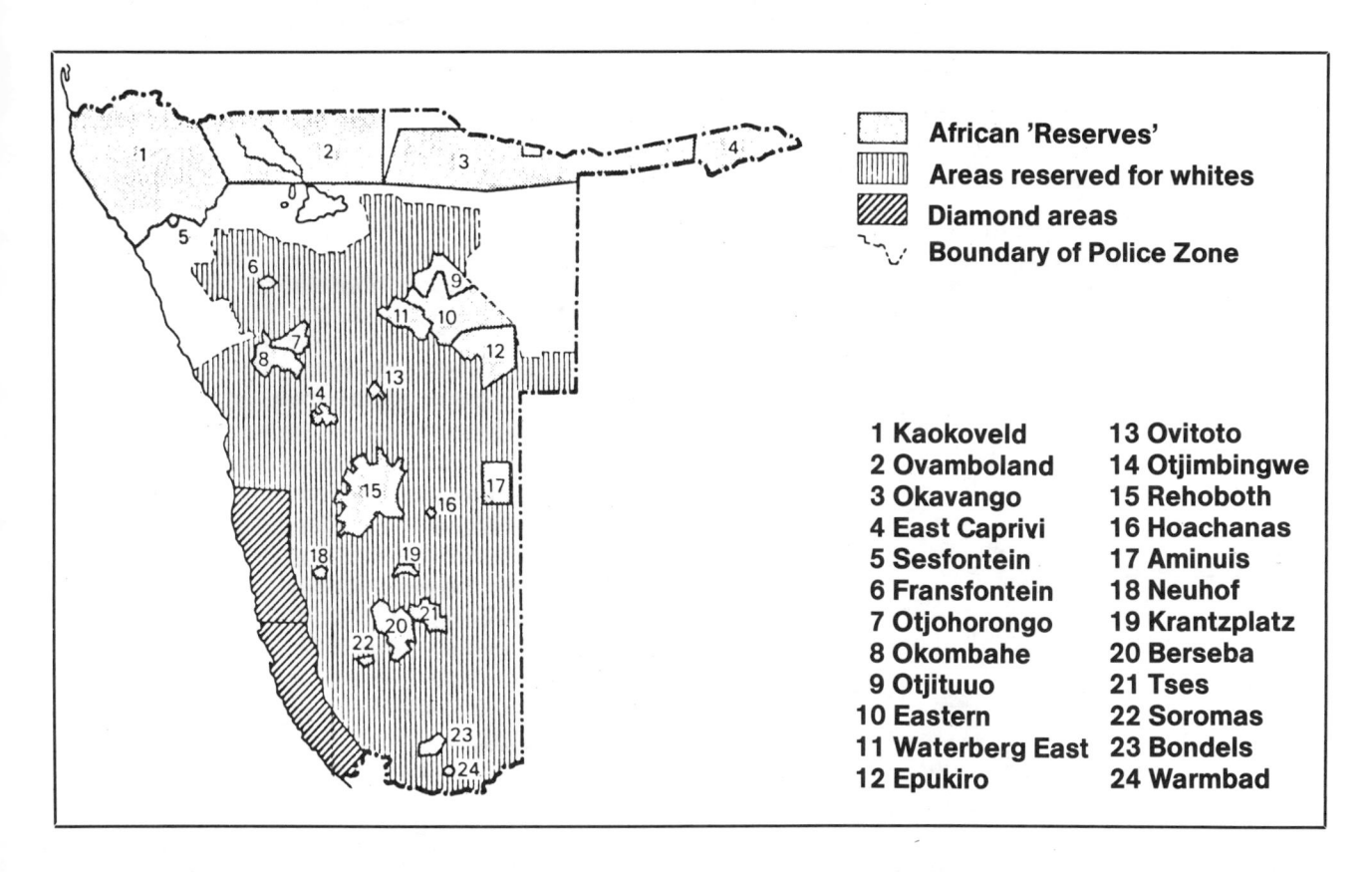

- African 'Reserves'
- Areas reserved for whites
- Diamond areas
- Boundary of Police Zone

1 Kaokoveld
2 Ovamboland
3 Okavango
4 East Caprivi
5 Sesfontein
6 Fransfontein
7 Otjohorongo
8 Okombahe
9 Otjituuo
10 Eastern
11 Waterberg East
12 Epukiro
13 Ovitoto
14 Otjimbingwe
15 Rehoboth
16 Hoachanas
17 Aminuis
18 Neuhof
19 Krantzplatz
20 Berseba
21 Tses
22 Soromas
23 Bondels
24 Warmbad

3) The 'homelands' according to the Odendaal-Plan

After the Boer Nationalist Party had introduced 'Apartheid' into South Africa as official policy in the early 1950s, the administration in Namibia some years later also started to re-organize the policy of 'divide and rule'. A commission was established in the early 1960s, named, after its chairman, the Odendaal-Commission. In 1964 this commission presented a report, in which it recommended the establishment of a so-called 'homeland' for each of the Namibian population groups. In the course of the implementation of this 'separate development' during the late 1960s, the Namibians were forcefully re-settled on a large scale (the experiences of the people are reported in more detail in a subsequent section of this book). The map on this page shows you the structure and distribution of the 'homelands' according to the Odendaal-Plan.

Tasks:
Compare the three maps and try to follow the historic stages, concerning the establishment of 'reserves' and 'homelands'.
If you have experience of daily life in these areas, share them with your classmates!
— *What makes the land-issue so important?*

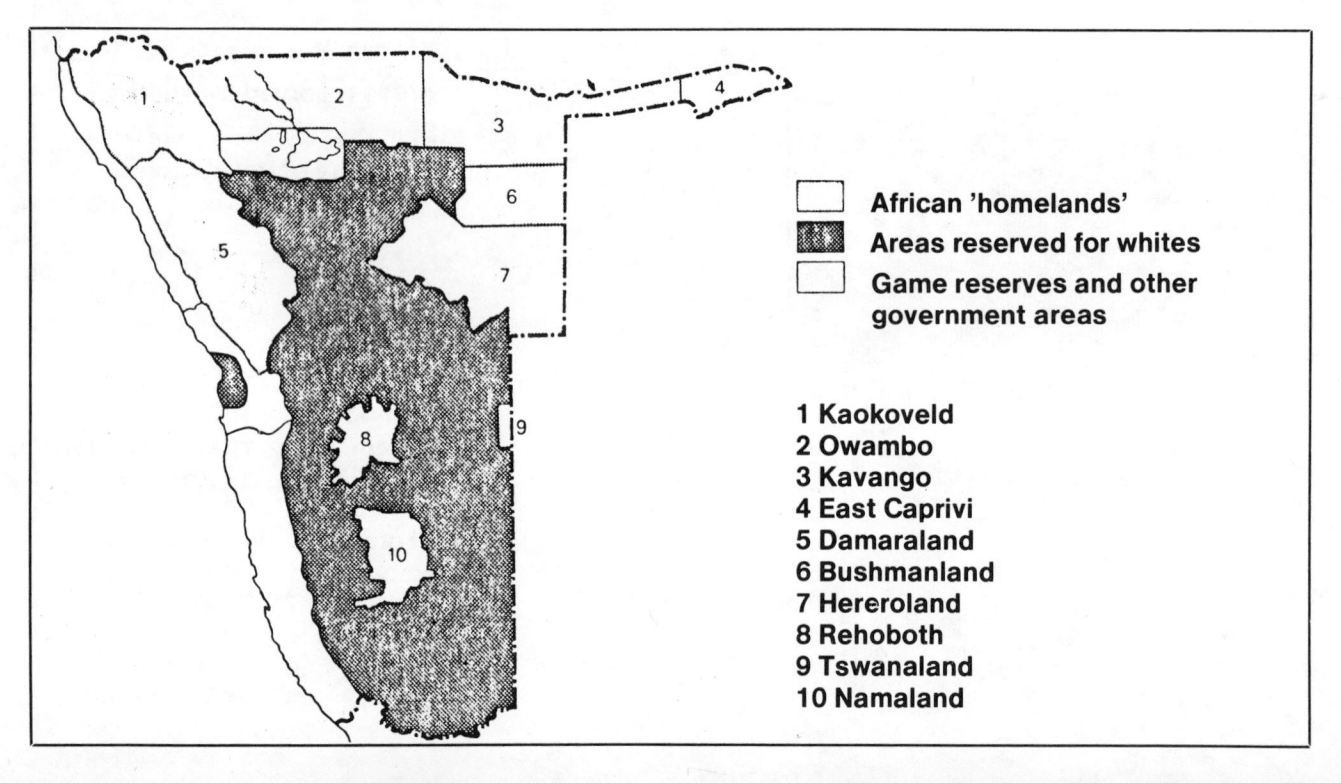

Legend:
- African 'homelands'
- Areas reserved for whites
- Game reserves and other government areas

1 Kaokoveld
2 Owambo
3 Kavango
4 East Caprivi
5 Damaraland
6 Bushmanland
7 Hereroland
8 Rehoboth
9 Tswanaland
10 Namaland

Part II:
OUR NAMIBIAN PAST – THE HISTORY OF OUR PEOPLE

Section 3

Before the white man came

Early nation-building: The peace-treaty of Hoachanas (1858)

From the notebook of an early European explorer (1895/1896)

The first land theft

From the diary of Hendrik Witbooi

Good old days

The poem on this page, written by a Namibian student at the United Nations Institute for Namibia, tries to remind us of the earlier times. Read it carefully and discuss its meaning. Try to find out what the writer wants to express with this poem. Tell each other, what you know about our country's past. When doing this also make use of information you can gather from other members of the community, mainly the elder people, who know some stories from former times.

BEFORE THE WHITE MAN CAME

Before the white man came
My people were the happiest nation
If I have to make any comparison
They were working hand in hand
eating from one plate
happy with one mother being close
sisters and brothers.

They had love from their motherland
They praised her for all she produced for them,
They had a surplus of almost everything
they needed.

We have to defend our motherland
with all her resources
To protect our children we have
to have weapons.
To maintain peace we must be strong.

But before they could be prepared
To defend their motherland
The white man came with a
stronger force than the grandparents
Could offer, they tried their level best
but couldn't conquer the brutality of the whites.

Their happiness was destroyed
They were forced to wage a very
arduous struggle. Now their blood is peeling
on the battle fields but determined
to fight to the bitter end to win
the happiness they had before
the white man came.

Shivute Shanumbundu

The picture below was drawn by an European traveller and early explorer, who came to Namibia in the middle of the 19th century. It shows a scene in Northern Namibia. — What do you see? Try to act out a play based on what you think the people in the picture are doing and saying. Also make drawings of your own, showing how you think the people were living at that time.

Early Nation-Building:

THE PEACE TREATY OF HOACHANAS (1858)

Already in the mid-19th century, the approaching colonial pressure from the Cape resulted in bitter fights among the Namibian tribes for power in central Namibia. The most outstanding leader during this period was Jonker Afrikaner, heading one of the Orlam tribes that had originally come from the Cape. Within a few years, Jonker Afrikaner managed to establish a powerful rule, under which many Orlam and Nama communities as well as part of the Herero came together to establish a new kind of intertribal relations. These efforts represented the first succesful moves towards the emergence of a Namibian nation.

Becoming aware of the increasing danger and threat the first whites represented, the local communities in the central and southern parts of Namibia came together for a meeting. In the course of this event, they decided upon a treaty for peace and friendship among each other with the aim of standing together against foreign influences and challenges.

Although in the future course of Namibian history this peace treaty of Hoachanas remained valid for a short time only, it remains an important document of the earlynation-building of our Namibian communities. The following passages are extracts from this treaty as agreed upon in 1858 and signed by such influential and important local leaders as Jonker Afrikaner, Kido Witbooi, Paul Goliath, Willem Swartbooi, Amraal, David Christian and Tjamuaha, while Maharero and a representative of the Griquas living in the northern Cape were also present.

Jonker Afrikaner

SETTLEMENT PATTERNS IN NAMIBIA (around 1840)

This map shows the settlement patterns of the Namibian communities around the middle of the 19th century in the central and southern part of our country.

Nearly all those communities living there and mentioned on this map were represented by their leaders at the conference in Hoachanas, which resulted in the peace treaty being agreed upon. The document was signed by the following leaders:

Cornelius Oasib Karab
Jager Aimab
Hendrik Hendrikes
!Nanib
Kido Witbooi A-lleib
Jonker Afrikaner
Itara-mub
Paul Goliath
Hobechab
Willem Swartbooi
Huiseb
Garib
Piet Kooper Gamab
Amraal Gai-Inub
David Christian
Naichab
Tjamuaha
Also present were:
Andries van Rooi
Maharero

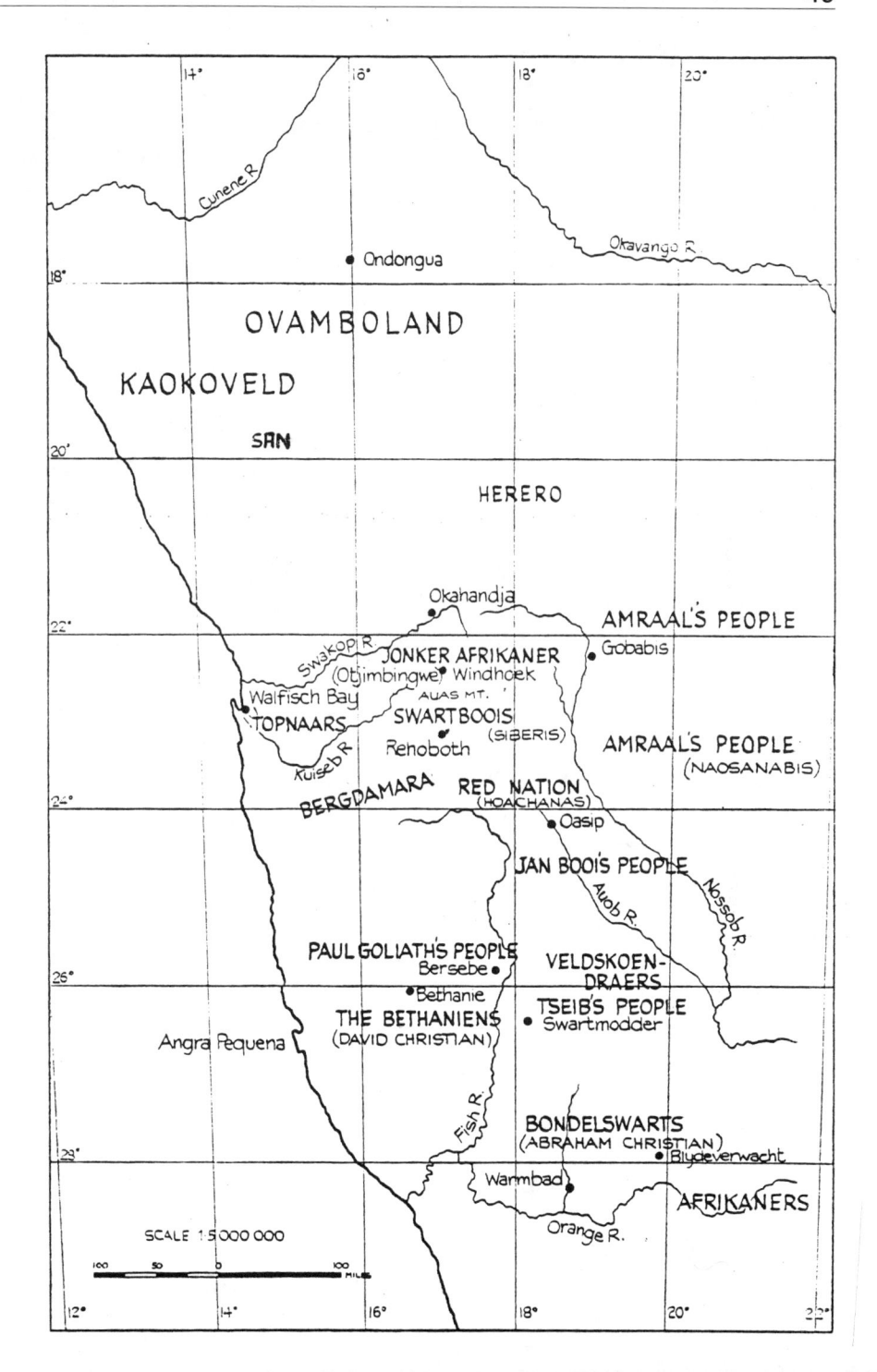

Peace Treaty of Hoachanas 1858

In the name of the Holy Trinity, the Father, the Son and the Holy Ghost, we the undersigned have resolved to unite in the following treaty:

Article 1: No chief with his people will have the right, should a dispute arise between him and another chief of standing, to pursue his own vindication, but shall be pledged to bring the case before an impartial court.

Article 2: When the case has been examined by the impartial chiefs, the guilty party shall be punished or a fine shall be imposed upon him. Should he be unwilling to comply with the judgement and should he attempt to dispute the issue by force of arms, then shall all the treaty chiefs be pledged jointly to take up arms and punish him.

Article 5: No chief may permit copper being mined in his territory without the knowledge and agreement of all other chiefs, or to sell a farm or site within his territory to a white person from the Cape Colony. Whoever despite this makes such a sale shall be heavily fined, and the purchaser himself will have to bear the cost if he has been acquainted with this law beforehand.

Article 6: We resolve also to close our bond and treaty with all Griqua chiefs. Should they need us in any major war which may befall their country, then we are ready to come to their assistance.

Article 8: No chief shall allow himself solely on account of rumours to become mistrustful and be prepared to take up arms without getting written proof thereof. Should this provision nevertheless be broken, the chief responsible will be heavily fined by the other chiefs.

Article 10: It is also resolved that each year a day and date will be agreed to consult together for the welfare of the land and the people.

Tasks:
From the excerpts of the peace treaty of Hoachanas you should be able to identify the important agreements made by the local chiefs. List them in your own words.
— Why, in your opinion, can this peace treaty be classified as one of the first major attempts at establishing a preliminary early nation?

FROM THE NOTEBOOK OF AN EARLY EUROPEAN EXPLORER (1895/1896)

Throughout the 19th century, Europeans travelled around our country to explore the characteristics of the people and their environment. They mostly put their observations down on record by writing diaries or similar reports - so-called travellogues. The insights they offer into the tribal societies were in some cases used by the colonial authorities to adapt their rule over the people to the local conditions existing.

Even today, these reports are one of the main sources of written information on this period of Namibian history, although their value is sometimes very limited. These Europeans (travellers, traders and missionaries) had narrow ideals of culture and civilisation, based exclusively on their own European way of life. They were in most cases unable to understand and accept different cultures and life-styles as strange but equal to the European one. Many of these reports therefore lack an honest and fair approach to our people. Nevertheless, an analysis of these reports - while bearing in mind their limitations - often proves to be useful for the exploration of our past.

In this chapter, we learn about one example of such reports: the notebook of a Swedish traveller with the name Möller. We have chosen some extracts from Möller's descriptions dealing with his impressions on a journey through Northern Namibia in 1895/1896. The original spelling of this time has been kept. There follow three paragraphs dealing with various aspects of the people's life in this region at the turn of the century.

This photo shows another Swede, living as a hunter and farmer in Namibia and accompanying Möller on some of his tours.

I. Manufacturing and trade

...weapons, as well as other objects of iron or copper of the Ovampo, are manufactured by themselves from local ore. They fetch the iron ore from the north and there are copper deposits southeast of Oundounga. The iron is smelted in small furnaces of clay in which ore and charcoal are packed in layers and through which a strong blast is produced by means of two bellows. The smiths, of which there appear to be several, particularly in Oukouanjama and Oukouambi, work with surprising skill despite the primitive tools. On my journey southwards to Damaraland I once camped at the same waterhole as a company of Oukouambi smiths and traders who were on their way to Damaraland, there to trade their ironware for cattle.

II. Agricultural Production

Agriculture is the main source of livelihood of the Ovampo people. Kaffircorn and millet are the principal kinds of grain. They also cultivate a kind of bean that grows below the soil; maize is also grown here and there, but tobacco occurs mainly among the northern tribes, Evari and Ehanda. The fields are carefully prepared for the sowing. Shortly before the rain period in October the women begin their work in the fields. The soil is fertilised with cattle manure and ash from the burnt remains from clearing land and the previous crop.

III. Settlement Habits

...in every village there are separate quarters for the girls and separate quarters for the young unmarried men; there are also a dancing place, a kraal for the cattle, a place where the corn is stamped to meal, and special places for the corn-baskets and for the churning of milk, everything according to a certain established system. The number of huts in every village varies from about twenty up to seventy. Among the various tribes the villages are differently situated in relation to the fields.
...After some years the village is moved, generally towards the east, and the old village place becomes a field.
The villages are surrounded by high palisades and thornbush hedges; with only one narrow entrance they can be regarded as small forts which are impenetrable by arrows and can well withstand a siege as long as water and food lasts.

Tasks:
List the activities and characteristics described above and try to find out what they represent with regard to the economic and social conditions. Consult other people outside the school, who remember stories about our past and the life of the people.
Try to do so also with regard to the people living at that time in other regions of our Namibian country and in other cultural communities.

What do you think are the limitations of such travellogues and what purposes did they serve? What other sources of information about our past do you know? What possibilities do we have to reconstruct the history of our country and our people?

These illustrations are taken from the notebook of another, British traveller, Sir Francis Galton, who visited Namibia in 1850 and 1851. Try to analyse the spirit in which these illustrations were made. What do you see, and (far more important) what do you miss in these pictures?

THE FIRST LAND THEFT

In early 1883 the German trader Adolph Lüderitz sent out his assistant Heinrich Vogelsang to acquire land along the coast of our country. This decision took place at a time when certain interest groups within Germany itself were enthusiastic about the idea of having colonies abroad. Vogelsang's mission had as its purpose the ultimate goal of creating the conditions necessary for declaring our Namibia as a German colony.

In April 1883, Vogelsang arrived by ship from the Cape at a bay on the Namibian coast which was called by the Portuguese Angra Pequena and later called Lüderitzbucht by the colonisers. In his diary, Vogelsang noted upon his arrival:

"After careful consideration Greater Namaqualand was chosen because not only can excellent business be done there in ostrich-feathers, cattle-breeding and trade, but also because rich copper mines are available in the interior there."

Vogelsang approached Joseph Fredericks, the chief of the local Bethanie-tribe, in whose possession the bay of Angra Pequena lay. On May 1st, 1883, he agreed with Fredericks upon a contract and purchased land to a distance of five miles around Angra Pequena.

This acquisition of land — and more contracts of a similar kind followed-caused enthusiasm in those German circles favouring the colonial dream.

In fact, only several months later, these possessions of Lüderitz served as the basis

Adolph Lüderitz (December 1885)

for the proclamation of our country as a German colony.

It is therefore important to know more about the 'legal basis' of these contracts: In all of them, the terms 'miles' or 'geographical miles' were used to identify and fix the size of land sold or purchased. Of course, the local people were only familiar with the English mile (about 1,600 metres). And the term 'mile' or 'geographical mile' used should just leave them in this belief! But afterwards, once the contracts were signed, Lüderitz and his agent claimed 'miles' referred to 'German miles', which had a length of nearly 7,500 metres and were completely unknown to the local people. Their chiefs even had maps in their hands in which the transfer of land had been marked in the course of the deals according to the length of the English miles!

In a letter to his employee Vogelsang, the trader Lüderitz gave orders to continue with this way of proceeding. On March 26th, 1884, he writes:

"Since it is stated in our purchasing contract ' = 20 geographical miles inland', we also wish to lay claim to the same. For the time being, let Joseph Fredricks believe that it concerns 20 English miles. Equally, buy the remaining coastline to 20 geographical miles inland at the same time."

This document proves that the acquisition of land by the German trader was based on deliberate fraud. Without knowing it, the local chiefs sometimes sold nearly all their tribal land to him! The 'legal' basis of German colonialism therefore turned out to be a simple theft, even according to the laws in existence within Germany herself.

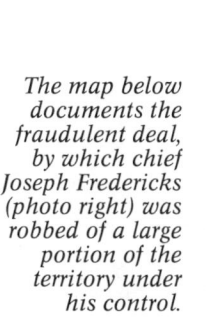

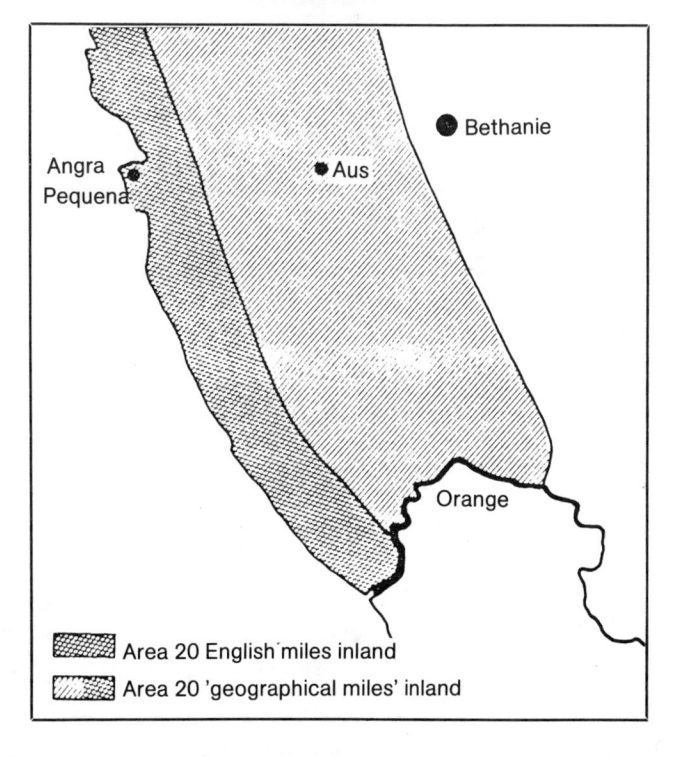

The map below documents the fraudulent deal, by which chief Joseph Fredericks (photo right) was robbed of a large portion of the territory under his control.

Area 20 English miles inland
Area 20 'geographical miles' inland

The first fraudulent contract of May 1st, 1883 (above left), which Heinrich Vogelsang (above right) initiated. A German eye-witnesses picture of the German flag being hoisted on August 7th, 1884, at Angra Pequena (below).

FROM THE DIARY OF HENDRIK WITBOOI (1884 – 1894)

This chapter presents some extracts from the diary of Hendrik Witbooi, one of our most prominent leaders in Namibian history.

Hendrik Witbooi, chief of the Nama when the Germans invaded our country, resisted the subjugation forced upon the people under the colonial system. His correspondence, which he kept as a kind of record in a collection (which he later on called his diary), is an impressive document of his attitude.

The letters written and received by Hendrik Witbooi were in Cape Dutch. After Hendrik Witbooi's defeat in 1894 by the German troops, these letters fell into the hands of the colonial masters.

The following five extracts from letters are documents from a very decisive period of colonisation and anti-colonial struggle in the early 1890s. They come from the time when pressure by the colonial authorities upon Hendrik Witbooi increased, to force him and his followers into one of the so-called protection treaties. Which, as a consequence, would have resulted in the loss of independence. The excerpts show that Hendrik Witbooi not only tried to resist this pressure as long as possible, but also that he realised the general threat to the other Namibian tribes. They also demonstrate his awareness of the nature of colonialism.

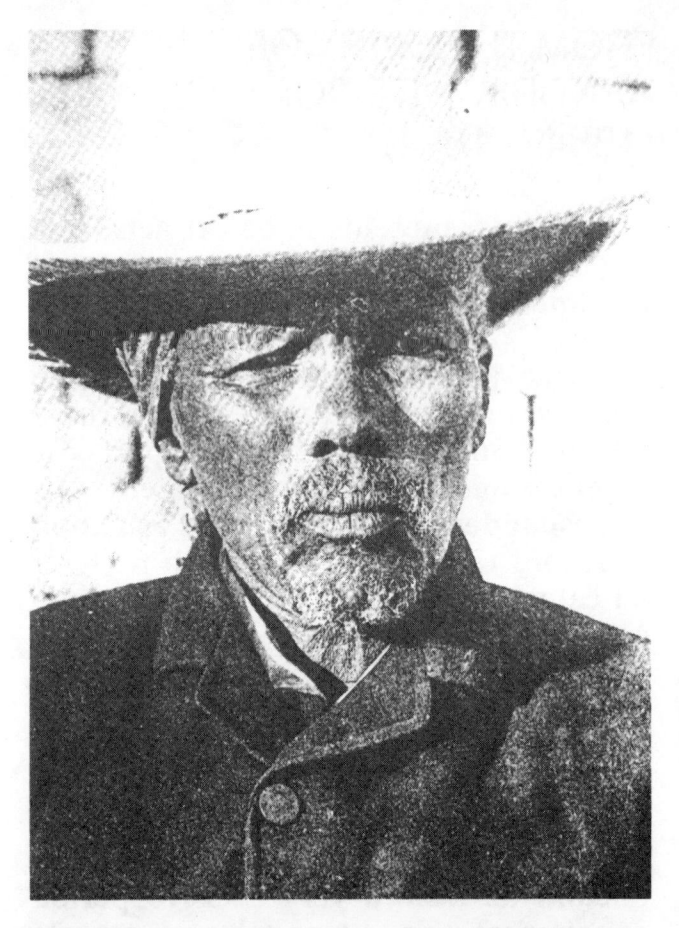

The diary of Hendrik Witbooi remains to this day one of the few genuine documents of African resistance to European colonialism taking place all over the African continent at that time. For our Namibian history it is an important source of information and a good example of the fighting spirit of those days.

On June 27th, 1892, Hendrik Witbooi expressed a grave warning to Chief Joseph Fredericks of Bethanie, who was the first of the local chiefs to sell land to Europeans and who later on agreed to a so-called protection treaty with the German Empire:

"I am very annoyed about you, captain of Great Namaqualand, who have accepted German protection and by doing so are giving the white people rights and influence in our country. I look at the affair with the Germans with completely different eyes. They pretend to protect you from other big nations. But it seems to me that they themselves are the big nation that intends to come by violence into our country.
I see them govern with violence and issue regulations which include prohibitions. Therefore, I don't wish you to hand over lands in our territory, on which these people are permitted to live, practise free rights and carry out work. Because of this, dear captain, be so kind and cancel this thing and don't allow white people to move onto your lands."

On August 4th, 1892, Hendrik Witbooi wrote to the British Magistrate based in Walfish Bay, to report to him his concern about German activities. He obviously hoped that the British might interfere (which, of course, they did not):

„I observe and hear things about the Germans which I dislike. They claim rights and activities also on my territory. I don't say anything, if they claim rights within the territories of those captains, who have placed themselves under their protection. But that they also come to my territory, although I did not place myself under their command,

Hendrik Witbooi in the company of his daughters, who became known as courageous and proud women.

this I cannot understand. The Germans pretend furthermore that they came to our country for the sake of peace. When looking at what they do, this claim does not seem to me to be the truth."

In a letter of August 7th, 1892, Hendrik Witbooi, on behalf of the Red Nation, issued another serious warning to Joseph Fredericks and appealed to him anew to stop the sell-out:
"As I've explained to you already in one of my first letters, it is usual among the captains of the red tribes, that our people live together at the same place conveniently, without obstacles, restrictions, difficulties or rivalry, and that we as captains can issue orders or make changes accordingly. With the Germans this is not the case; therefore I don't wish you to grant them still further rights in our country. I am of the opinion, that you captains who have placed yourself under German protection, should all consider how good and useful it coult still become for you, that I as captain have yet excluded myself, my people and land."

As a response to the colonial threat, the various tribes intensified their contact with each other on a more cooperative basis, instead of fighting each other for military superiority within the region. Among the Nama and Herero, the increasing danger of losing their independent authority led to communication and an arrangement between the old rivals Hendrik Witbooi and Maharero, who were willing to resist together the growing pressure. Proof of these efforts is a letter, in which Maharero responds to a note received from Hendrik Witbooi. On November 1st, 1892, he writes back to the Nama chief:

„Furthermore, I've learnt here that the Boers plan to move into your country. Remember this and don't allow them to pass your territory, so that they don't come here or settle there at your places. Make every effort to prevent them from entering and don't wait until the whole country is crowded with them."

**But the resistance to the colonial monster was in vain. When the Germans started to put pressure on Hendrik Witbooi to end his independent chieftainship and to force him into a so-called protection treaty with the colonial authority, they first cut him off from his supply of ammunition and then attacked him.
Hendrik Witbooi was in a bad position, but still not prepared to give up, as his letter of July 24th, 1893, to the commander of the German troops shows:**

If you have in mind to continue fighting me, then, my dear friend, I shall have to ask you to share two cases of bullets with me, so that I'll be able to answer your attack. I have not really fought with you yet. You have withheld my ammunition and attacked me. Release the ammunition, as suits a big, honest, civilized nation.
As soon as I am in possession of enough

ammunition, you can defeat me. Only then, could this mean a great, honest victory to your big nation."

But it took only a few months longer. Then the Nama, under their chief Hendrik Witbooi, finally had to sign a treaty with the Germans, which forced them to submit to the foreign authority and took away their independence. They were moved to a reservation at Gibeon. Hendrik Witbooi remained there for more than ten years and seemed to be a broken man.

> Tasks:
> *Try to find out about the values and ideas Hendrik Witbooi had, as they are expressed in the above extracts from some of his letters.*
> *Why do you think it is so important to read and learn about former times by means of such documents as the diary of Hendrik Witbooi?*
> *What other sources of history do you know of?*
> *Compare them with each other and discuss their advantages and limitations.*

Hendrik Witbooi with his troops after signing a treaty with the Germans.

> This poem takes up the history of our people before we were colonised and compares the past with the present. The memories it brings to us draw a beautiful picture of our past, while today we are suffering.

> **Tasks:**
> *Compare the poem with the illustration and identify the messages of both. Then remember what you've learnt about the history of our people before foreigners came to Namibia.*
> *Discuss, whether we should try to go back to the old days when independent, or if it would be better if we looked to the future. Discuss further, what you think should be remembered from the old days and be kept alive and be integrated into our new society. List the topics you think are important for an independent Namibia, and how these topics are related to the experiences of the past. At the same time, identify the challenges ahead of us, which we never had to cope with in the history of our country before we were colonised.*

GOOD OLD DAYS

I lived peacefully
Under the rule of my kings
Moved freely and confidently
Up and down the country
Without let of hindrance

The country was ours
In our name and right
We occupied the land
The forests, the rivers and the like
We set up and operated our Government
We organised our trade and commerce

Since the advent of colonialism
Since the advent of imperialism
My good days are striked down
The land dispossessed
Racists dominate

I am now embarrassed
No more moving freely
No more up and down the country
No more land

The colonialists deny me all these
Imperialism, apartheid deny me all these
Good old days

Geraldt Tjozongoro

Part II:
OUR NAMIBIAN PAST – THE HISTORY OF OUR PEOPLE

Section 4

The German colonial ideology

The mentality of white masters

**Anti-colonial resistance:
Chief Kambonde**

The German-Namibian War:
— Samuel Maharero's initiative
— The extermination of the Herero nation
— The South stands up
— Jacob Marengo — Profile of a Namibian leader

White opposition to colonial practices

**Some old people remember their history:
King Mandume of Northern Namibia**

The old Namibian peasant

Consequences of defeat: The origins of apartheid

The change of masters: South African rule

THE GERMAN COLONIAL IDEOLOGY

In 1884 the German Empire declared overseas territories to be under her colonial rule and thereby made the people living there colonial subjects. The mentality behind this move was characterised by the so-called „civilising spirit". Similar to what had happened within the societies of other colonial powers, those supporting colonialism within Germany tried to use various arguments to legitimate the seizure of foreign land and people. Some of these arguments follow in this section. They show that those Germans in favour of colonialism possessed what could be called a "superiority complex". Three slightly different but typical positions on colonialism are documented.

The most general one in terms of moral justification and glorification was expressed in a very typical fashion by an author writing books for German children. In one of those books, published in 1894, he praised the colonial activities of Germany in the following way:

"German eagerness and German energy have gained an important field of activity. Now it is their task to make these countries accessible, to lead those, who are descended into barbarism, upward towards brighter heights of morality."

This position takes European culture as the one and only civilisation. Other ways of living were not accepted as tolerable. Colonial activities therefore were considered to be the civilising task necessary for the benefit of the colonised people. On the basis of this definition, which attests a moral obligation to the culturally superior European way of life, the domination of other people was justifiable.

But, of course, the claimed moral aspects were just a disguise for other motives, which could be identified as economic interest in the exploitation of the countries and peoples under occupation.

One of the most prominent representatives of a very conservative colonial ideology was Paul Rohrbach. During the early years of this century he was serving as an official commissioner of the German authorities in Namibia, being responsible for the settlement of Germans.

For him, there was no doubt that, on the basis of an assumed higher moral and civilised position of Europeans, they had the right to destroy the original way of life of the colonised African people:

„The decision to colonise in South Africa means nothing less than that the Native tribes must withdraw from the lands on which they have pastured their cattle and so let the White man pasture his cattle on the selfsame lands. If the moral right of this standpoint is questioned, the answer is that, for people of the cultural standard of South African natives, the loss of their free national barbarism and the development of a class of workers in the service of and dependent on the Whites is primarily a law of existence in the highest degree. For a people, as for an individual, an existence appears to be justified in the degree to which it is useful in the progress of general development. By no argument in the world can it be shown that the preservation of any degree of national independence, national prosperity, and political organisation by the races of South West Africa would be of greater or even equal advantage for the development of mankind in general or German people in particular than that these races should be made serviceable in the enjoyment of their former territories by the White races."

Gloryfying illustrations like this one of a German colonial soldier were typical of the colonial enthusiasm prevailing.

This position already emphasises the economic motives behind the morally disguised arguments.
In contrast to this reactionary and hypocritical statement, there was a faction of colonial supporters who did not try to cover the true reasons. Theodor Leutwein, between 1894 and 1904 the first German governor of Namibia, held such a position to be somehow more honest. His judgement about the aims of colonialism at least doesn't pretend that it is based on humanitarian grounds:

„The final aim of each and every colonisation is — stripped of all its idealistic and humanitarian accessories — finally just simple business. The colonising race does not intend to bring the possibly expected fortune to the indigenous population of the country to be colonised. Instead it is in the first instance looking for its own advantage... With regard to the way of colonisation there is consequently basically only one guiding principle, namely the one which leads most safely towards the aspired business."

Tasks:
In this topic you have been confronted with three positions typical of the period of German colonialism. These positions, in different ways and on various levels, highlight the colonial ideology represented within the German empire.
— *Summarise in your own words the basic meaning of the statements quoted.*
— *Compare the arguments with each other, look for similarities and differences.*
— *Which were the pretended or assumed justifications given for colonialism?*
— *What do you think were the real motives behind the arguments?*

This front cover of the German magazine "Colony and Home" is typical for the colonial ideology of these days: It shows people from the various German colonies hailing the German emperor.

THE MENTALITY OF WHITE MASTERS

Most of the Germans coming to Namibia after it was declared a colony of the German empire represented in one way or another the German colonial ideology already referred to. As individuals, they shared attitudes about themselves and the people they were colonising. A few of these individual attitudes are quoted to give you an insight.

In 1912, a book was published in Germany, containing letters from a German settler woman in Namibia. In this book, this woman writes about her experiences as the wife of a farmer and also deals with the African people she had been confronted with. One of her statements shows the ignorance of her perspective, which denies the Africans of the time any human nature:

„What do we know about the past of this country? Thousands of years of deepest ignorance passed over it. People, living until the present day like animals, dwelt in the grasslands and mountain nooks. They lived and perished without realising any sense of life."

A racial superiority-complex made white settlers like this woman believe that black people were not members of human mankind but instead had more in common with animals.

Many of these settlers believed therefore, that these black people first of all would have to be trained to become members of the human race.

When at the turn of the century, members of the German parliament discussed the cruelties in the colonies and especially the question of corporal punishment, 75 German settlers in Namibia sent a petition to the German parliament in July 1900, in which they argued:

One of the early German farmers.

„From time immemorial our natives have grown used to laziness, brutality and stupidity. The dirtier they are, the more they feel at ease. Any white man who has lived among natives finds it almost impossible to regard them as human beings at all in any European sense. They need centuries of training as human beings, with endless patience, strictness and justice..."

And in 1908, one of the most influential farmers in Namibia expressed in a speech before the local colonial administration the general feeling among the settlers of the time by declaring:

„Our policies will therefore be those of masters. We shall make people realise that we Germans are the masters of the country, and the natives the servants whose welfare depends on the advantage of their masters."

These experiences recently influenced one of our fellow-Namibians to write a short essay, adressing the West German public of today. In it he deals with the historic experience of our people under German rule and reaches the following conclusion:

„When I think of the history of my people, think of what we have had to suffer from the Europeans, then I can only say, you should have kept your so-called culture to yourselves. They tried to destroy our identity, to cultivate us to slavery. I believe as atrocious as genocide is the mental murdering that was to have been carried out on us — in the name of humanity and occidental culture."

Tasks:
This topic deals — in addition to the one presented before — with the colonial mentality of the white settlers as individuals.
— Compare the attitudes expressed in the documents with those presented earlier.
— Do you find any differences?
— Summarise in your own words the basic meaning of the statements quoted.
— Comment on the articulated positions. Write down your own conclusions. Are they similar to those expressed by the fellow-Namibian quoted in this topic?
— Find out to what extent you have experienced similar attitudes under the present colonial system personally.
— How much has changed in the mind of the white settlers and how much do you still think the old colonial mind is still alive?

The photos on these pages give you an impression of the appearance of those settlers living in our country at the turn of the century.

ANTI-COLONIAL RESISTANCE: CHIEF KAMBONDE

When looking into old books and reports dating from the time of the German occupation of our country, we sometimes find very interesting stories about the resistance of the local Namibians to the new power established. One of these examples is described in this section which deals with an event in 1902, in which the famous chief Kambonde from Northern Namibia showed his firm rejection of foreign rule.

During this time, in 1902, there were rumours in Ovamboland, that the Germans planned to build a railway through Northern Namibia. To create the possibility, they intended to send an army to Ovamboland to show their strength. The people living there were therefore very much concerned.

In this tense atmosphere, a young Briton looking for minerals entered Northern Namibia, accompanied by two fellow-travellers from England. They did so at their own risk, as the German authorities were not prepared to offer them security forces.

The three finally arrived on territory controlled by the Ovambo, where the Germans had as yet little or no influence. To show their neutrality, they put a British flag on their cart. But one of them had a German-sounding name and was therefore banned from entering Chief Kambonde's kraal. The other two were allowed to do so, but people remained suspicious. Only after a few days, when they could be sure that they were British and not working for the Germans, they were offered the general hospitality of the Ovambo.

Chief Kambonde, realising the chance offered by the presence of the Britons, asked them to help him in his efforts to protest against the German actions. The visitors suggested that he writes a letter which they would then carry to the Governor of the Cape Colony. This Chief Kambonde did, and the English translation the visitors took along finally sounded as follows:

"Karoka, Ovamboland,
December 22nd, 1902

Honoured Sir,

I, Kambonde, Chief Captain of the Ovambo nation, south of the Kunene river, send you greetings.
I am in trouble. My people number many thousands. They are all workers. They till the soil; and are not a burden on any people. The Germans who have a Government at Windhoek are encroaching upon my territory. I learn that they also say that my territory belongs to them. They offered me much money for my country. I refused... My people are armed with English rifles. I shall resist the Germans... Englishmen who call themselves a company tell the Ovambo people that they work for the English Government. They want to build a railway through my country, and I have learned that they have

lied to me, and that they are under the German Government. If the railway is built it will bring the German soldiers and taxes on my people. I will not have it. I will fight to the last man. Do you approve of those Englishmen who thus lie to me and my people, and do these things in England's name? I want your help at once. Send me word by messenger. The Germans open my letters otherwise."

This letter was sent on by the Governor in Cape Town to the Colonial Office in London, but there it was only put into a file and no reaction followed. Nevertheless, Chief Kambonde and his people showed such strength that the Germans were hesitant for all the years they were in colonial power to establish direct rule based on military violence in Northern Namibia.

A palisaded village in Ovamboland.

THE GERMAN–NAMIBIAN WAR

At the turn of the century, the colonial system imposed upon the Namibian people increased in pressure and threatened their existence. More settlers entered our country and tried to get hold of as much land and cattle as possible by the cheapest means. This was only to be realised to the disadvantage of the Namibians. The efforts of the settlers concentrated on the central and southern parts of our country, where the land was best suited for cattle-ranching and where — as a consequence of this — the Namibian communities of Nama and Herero were grazing their herds.

Whites expropriated the Namibians by various fraudulent deals. Among the most popular ones were those of trade. Often, white traders simply unloaded their goods at a certain place and left again. Afterwards, they would return and claim that they would still have to receive payment for the goods they left. With the help of the administration, they then took the land and cattle from the Namibians. 1902, for example, was named by the Herero "ojovuronde juviuego", which means the year of traders and fraud.

The conditions for survival on the basis of the traditional way of life were threatened among the Nama and Herero communities. It became increasingly obvious that only armed resistance against the colonial regime would prevent the people from being completely robbed and forced under a system they did not want. Instead of accepting the alternative offered, to live as workers for the white settlers under miserable conditions, the Namibians decided to take up arms and to fight for the maintenance of their original way of living.

This had already happend several times before, since the Germans had declared Namibia a colony. But the actions always took place on a very limited regional scale and were no real challenge to the militarily superior colonial system. Now, in early 1904, when the Herero rose, they did so on a well organised, unified basis. In the same year, the communities in the South under the leadership of Hendrik Witbooi decided on the same. We can therefore classify the military actions taking place between 1904 and 1907 as a first kind of national liberation struggle, which even included smaller actions of resistance from the Ovambo living in the North, so far relatively untouched by the colonial administration. In this section, some authentic documents from the German-Namibian war are presented.

1) Samuel Maharero's initiative

In the weeks before war started, Samuel Maharero as paramount chief of the Herero made contact with the people and their leaders. To Hermanus van Wyk, head of the Rehobother Baster community, he wrote:

"I would rather that they (the Germans) annihilate us and take over our lands than to go on as we are."

Samuel Maharero

To Hendrik Witbooi, he adressed the following letter (which was not delivered but handed over to the Germans instead by the messenger):

"All our obedience and patience with the Germans avails us nothing. My brother, do not go back on your word and stay out of the fighting, but rather let all the people fight against the Germans and let us be resolved to die together rather than to be killed by the Germans through mistreatment, imprisonment, or some other way. Further, you should inform all your captains who are subject to you that they too should stand and fight."

To the son of Chief Zacharias of Otjimbingwe Maharero sent a message saying:
"Your father knows that if we rebel we will be annihilated in battle since our people are practically unarmed and without ammunition, but the cruelty and injustice of the Germans have driven us to despair and our leaders and our people both feel that death has lost its terrors because of the conditions under which we now live."

Finally, before starting the decisive struggle for survival, Maharero issued the following order to his combatants:
"I am the principal chief of the Hereros. I have proclaimed the law and the just word, and I mean for all my people. They should not lay hands on any of the following: Englishmen, Basters, Berg Damaras, Namas and Boers. On none of these shall hands be laid. I have pledged my honour that this thing shall not take place. Nor shall the missionaries be harmed."

Further more, he also prohibited the killing of women and children. With only very few exceptions, these orders were strictly respected and followed by the fighting Herero.

When war was declared against the German colonialists (and only they were the target) in late January 1904, the Germans were surprised by the actions taken. It therefore took some months time, before the colonial administration was finally in a position of military strength again and managed to react with unrestricted violence.

From the German empire, thousands of soldiers and sophisticated weaponry were shipped to the Namibian colony. Based on this military superiority, a terrible war machine finally started to spread destruction among the Namibian people who had dared to resist.

2) The extermination of the Herero nation

The officer appointed in command of the German troops already had his "merits" collected prior to the outbreak of the German-Namibian war. In the German-East African colony, he was one of those officers who brutally surpressed the resistance by the local Wahehe people. And in China, he commanded German troops who destroyed the Chinese resistance to German colonial rule.

These "merits" finally resulted in appointing him for the mission of military command over the German troops fighting the Herero. The name of this commander with the mentality of a butcher was von Trotha. Before taking up his position in Namibia, he had once noted in a letter: "I destroy the rebellious natives by rivers of money and rivers of blood..."

German soldiers shortly before being shipped to Namibia.

Already in August 1904, the Herero were in the defensive. They all assembled at the Waterberg to face the decisive battle with the German enemy. Thereby, they offered the Germans the opportunity to apply the superiority in arms and number of professionally trained soldiers efficiently. Consequently, within days, the battle at the Waterberg broke the armed resistance of the Herero decisively. But von Trotha was not satisfied with this victory. A defeat of the Herero was not enough, he wanted the destruction of the Herero people. On October 2nd, 1904, von Trotha issued a proclamation, which afterwards became known as an extermination order:

"I, the great general of the German troops, send this letter to the Herero people. Hereros are no longer German subjects. ... All the Hereros must leave the land. If the people do not do this, then I will force them to do it with the great guns. Any Herero found within the German borders with or without a gun, with or without cattle, will be shot. I shall no longer receive any women or children; I will drive them back to their people or I will shoot them. This is my decision for the Herero people.
The Great General of the Mighty Kaiser"

Following this order, the German troops started to hunt for helpless Herero. — The horrifying reality of these days is even read behind the words and phrases noted in the official records of the German high command published after the event:

Von Trotha (left) tried to destroy the Herero nation: Below a view of the Waterberg to the east, where the dry Omaheke stretches.

"This bold enterprise shows up in the most brilliant light the ruthless energy of the German command in pursuing their beaten enemy. No pains, no sacrifices were spared in eliminating the last remnants of enemy resistance. Like a wounded beast the enemy was tracked down from one water-hole to the next, until finally he became the victim of his own environment. The arid Omaheke was to complete what the German army had begun: the extermination of the Herero nation."

A German soldier, member of the colonial troops, wrote down in a letter the following impressions during the persuance of the defeated Herero:

"Through the quiet night we heard, in the distance, the lowing of enormous herds of thirsty cattle, and a dull, confused sound like the movement of a whole people. To the east there was a gigantic glow of fire. The enemy had fled to the east with their whole enormous mass — women, children, and herds.

The next morning we ventured to pursue the enemy. The ground was trodden down into a floor for a width of about a 100 yards, for in such a broad thick horde had the enemy and their herds of cattle stormed along. In the path of their flight lay blankets, skins, ostrich feathers, household utensils, women's ornaments, cattle, and men — dead and dying and staring blankly...

A number of babies lay helplessly langui-

Captured Herero

shing by mothers whose breasts hung down long and flabby. Others were lying alone, still living, with eyes and nose full of flies. Somebody sent out our black drivers and I think they helped them to die. All this life lay scattered there, both men and beasts, broken in the knees, helpless, still in agony, or already motionless. ...

At noon we halted by waterholes which were filled to the brim with corpses. We pulled them out with ox teams but there was only a little stinking bloody water in the depth... At some distance crouched a crowd of old women who started in apathy... In the last frenzy of despair man and beast will plunge wildly into the bush somewhere, anywhere, to find water and in the bush they will die of thirst."

One Namibian, at this time serving the German troops, later on reported about the atrocities taking place during the course of war:

"She was quite a young woman and looked tired and hungry. Von Trotha asked her several questions, but she did not seem inclined to give information. She said her people had all gone towards the east, but as she was a weak woman she could not keep up with them. Von Trotha then ordered that she should be taken aside and bayoneted. I took the woman away, and a soldier came up with his bayonet in his hand. He offered it to me and said I had better stab the woman. I said I would never dream of doing such a thing, and asked why the poor woman could not be allowed to live. The

Almost starved Herero who survived the battle at Waterberg.

soldier laughed and said, "If you won't do it I will show you what a German soldier can do". He took the woman aside a few paces and drove the bayonet through her body. He then withdrew the bayonet and brought it, all dripping with blood, and poked it under my nose in a jeering way, saying, "you see, I have done it". Officers and soldiers were standing around looking on, but no one interfered to save the woman... On our return journey we again halted at Hamakari. There near a hut we saw an old Herero woman of about 50 or 60 years, digging in the ground for wild onions. Von Trotha and his staff were present. A soldier jumped off his horse and shot the woman through the forehead at point blank range. Before he shot her he said "I am going to kill you". She simply looked up and said "I thank you". I was an eyewitness of everything I have related... I was for nearly two years with the German troops, an always with General Von Trotha. I know of no instance in which prisoners were spared."

3) The South stands up

The communities in the south, hesitant until mid-1904 to join the Herero in their struggle, were aware of the cruelties committed by the German troops. This and the knowledge of the increasing hate of the settlers towards all Namibians finally brought them to decide on the same course the Herero had taken, although at this time these people had already been decisively beaten.

Hendrik Witbooi, of whose resistance and final subjugation in the course of the 1890s we've already learnt about in a previous section, rose up once again after ten years of peace with the Germans. As the undisputed leader in the south, his decision was the signal to nearly all the Nama communities to join the war against the German foreigners.

On October 1st, 1904, Hendrik Witbooi wrote to the other captains of the Nama communities:

"My sons, as we all know for a long time I have lived under the law, and in the law, just as we all have in the hope that God

Transport of Herero prisoners.

the Father would determine the time to free us from the difficulties of this world. For I have borne everything with peace and patience and I have endured everything that oppressed my heart because I waited for the Lord. Now I will not waste many words. ...
I have now stopped walking submissively and will write a letter to the Captain (of the German authorities) saying that I have put on the white feather (the sign for time of war) and that the time is over when I will walk behind him. The time has expired and the Saviour himself will now act and he will free us through his grace and compassion."

More than seventy years of age, Hendrik Witbooi fought his final battle. In small units on speedy horses, the Nama operated against the Germans with a very

The arrogance of power: A German post card with Nama prisoners of war as motive (note the many children).

efficient guerilla-strategy, fooling the clumsy enemy.

During one of the many attacks, Hendrik Witbooi was severely wounded and finally died. But his body never fell into the hands of the white invaders. He was burried secretly at a place not known to any white until this day.

Von Trotha, the German officer in command of the colonial army, issued another proclamation, this time addressing the Nama people.

On April 21st, 1905, he once more proved his butcher's mentality by writing:

"... those few who do not submit will suffer the same fate that befell the Hereros, who in their blindness believed that they could carry on successful war with the mighty German Emperor and the great German people. ...

The Hottentots will suffer the same fate if they do not surrender and give up their weapons.

... He who believes that mercy will not be extended to him should leave the land for as long as he lives on German soil he will be shot – this policy will go on until all such Hottentots have been killed."

In 1911, in the course of a population census, about 15,000 Herero out of an estimated number of 80,000 prior to the war were registered, while the number of Nama amounted to 10,000 out of an original 20,000. This means, that no fewer than 80 per cent of the Herero and 50 per cent of the Nama had thus fallen victim to German colonial rule.

4) Jacob Marengo – Profile of a Namibian leader

Jacob Marengo — in many sources and reports incorrectly referred to as Morenga — was a new kind of Nambian leader emerging from the time of resistance to the colonial system. Rooted by descent both in the Nama and Herero communities and not a traditional chief, he himself already symbolized a new personality and embodiment of Herero-Nama unity in their common action against German occupation.

In the course of the struggle, Marengo turned out to be the most skillful and clever guerilla-fighter, leading one of the most highly trained of all guerilla-units, originally composed of only eleven men from both the Herero and Nama. Within half a year, his following increased to 400 of the best trained men.

From mid-1904 onward, Marengo and his units managed to challenge the German troops succesfully for three years by making effective use of the local environment. The Karras mountains, offering them natural shelter, served as the base for their operations. At the same time, advantage was taken of the colonial boundary, separating Namibia and the South African territory under British rule. If necessary, Marengo and his units entered South African territory to escape German pursuit. In the beginning, the British tolerated this tactic. Later on, Marengo's military success made them afraid that it might stimulate the local South African people, who were much in sympathy with Marengo's struggle, to take up arms against British rule as well.

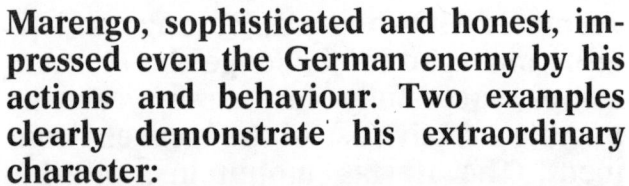

A view of the Karras mountains (above), which served as a base for Marengo's military operations. There he also received representatives of the German colonial regime for negotiations (right).

Marengo, sophisticated and honest, impressed even the German enemy by his actions and behaviour. Two examples clearly demonstrate his extraordinary character:

In October 1904, his unit attacked German troops based at a place called Wasserfall. He got hold of the station's horses and thereby made it impossible for the Germans to move with great speed from one location to another. But the horses Marengo captured were in bad condition. Marengo therefore sent a letter to the nearest German command in which he complained about the ill-treatment and bad feeding of these horses, as he had no use for such halfstarved creatures.

Marengo's treatment of and respect for captured German soldiers was as extraordinary as his conduct of war. In spite of being aware of all the atrocities committed by the German troops, Marengo always respected the enemy soldiers as human beings. For example, after he won a victory at Jerusalem over the German post based there, he informed the German command of what had taken place and asked them "to send a doctor for the wounded German soldiers".

Marengo was finally defeated only through the combined efforts of the German and British colonial authorities. When, in September 1907, he once more stayed in British-South African territory near the border of his country Namibia, he was shot by British soldiers. — But in the memory of our Namibian people he is still alive as one of the new kind of leaders emerging out of the anti-colonial struggle early this century.

In 1906, Jacob Marengo was arrested by the British in South Africa after again crossing the border from Namibia to seek shelter. On this occasion, a newspaper correspondent did an interview, later published in the Cape Times of May 29, 1906:

— Where were you captured?
— I was captured six miles inside British territory.
— What were you doing in British territory?
— I brought the women and children over for safety, and I had a number of men with me, but we were all unarmed, and the Germans fired upon us, and killed 27 of my men in British territory. We made no resistance, as we did not come to fight in British territory.
— Did you get wounded?
— Yes, I got wounded in my head, and the mark of the wound is here on my head, as you will observe from the scar.
— How long have you been fighting?
— I have been fighting for two years and five months.
— Have you any food supplies in your country?
— No, we live from the supplies we capture from the Germans, which are plentiful.
— Do you think this war will continue long?
— Yes, certainly, as long as there is a man on the field.
— Do you know that Germany is one of the mightiest military powers in the world?
— Yes, I am aware of it; but they cannot fight in our country. They do not know where to get water, and do not understand guerilla warfare.

Marengo with members of his guerilla-unit. The photo was probably taken in early 1907 during his exile in the Cape colony.

– Why did you commence warfare?
– Because I consider the Germans treated us cruelly, like dogs, and we would not stand it, but rather fight and die, as there is no justice for us.
– Where were you previous to the war?
– I worked for some time in the copper mines at O'Kiep, Namaqualand.
– Is it true that you shot the Germans after you captured them?
– No, I did not do so. I disarmed them, and sent them back."

The correspondent reporting on the interview further stated in his article:
"I understand that Marengo was educated by a missionary, and travelled for 18 months with him in Europe. He appears very shrewd and intelligent, and has a splendid physique. He is very gentlemanly in his conversation. His answers are straight.
Marengo's appearance does not show any despondency, and he looks in good health. Your correspondent offered him some cigars which he took eagerly, and when he went up to the railway station... he smoked a cigar, and looked quite happy and contented. Marengo said that his commando consisted of only 115 men fighting, and that only small commandoes were fighting the Germans."

Other prominent leaders of the early period of broad resistance were:
— Simon Kopper, who kept on fighting until 1908 and finally died in exile in Bechuanaland in January 1913.
— Abram Morris, who together with his brother and Jakobus Christiaan was among the closest followers and most experienced fighters of Marengo's unit. After Marengo's final defeat, Abram Morris and Jakobus Christiaan settled in exile at a place near the South African-Namibian border. Both of them returned to our country after the Germans had to give up Namibia in the course of World War I.
About 50 years of age, Abram Morris returned in 1922 to his Bondelzwarts community and once again — this time against the new South African rulers — together with Jakobus Christiaan, led the people to fight by armed resistance the high taxes forced upon them. He fell in battle as the last of those who, in 1904, brought the new Namibian nation, by their war of liberation, into existence.

Tasks:
When you have read all the documents of this section on the German-Namibian war, discuss the topic of war on a general level:
— Why has there been war?
— For what reasons can a war take place?
— What could be the aim of a war?
— What wars do you know about?

WHITE OPPOSITION TO COLONIAL PRACTICES

Not all Germans supported the brutal colonial subjugation of our Namibian people, although the majority of Germans sympathised in one way or another with the colonial idea. This even included most members of the Social Democratic Party, who did not fundamentally object to colonialism as such, but only to certain colonial practices.

Nevertheless, as the following excerpt from a speech by August Bebel, leader of the Social Democrats in the German parliament shows, the policy of colonialism was in any case a much debated issue. Commenting on the plans to build a railway line from the copper deposits and mines at Otavi through land in the possession of the Herero (one of the factors finally resulting in the German-Namibian War), August Bebel stated:

"The Hereros have already been robbed of a large part of their land and have had to move further east. But if they now hear that the new railroad construction is planned which, according to their experience thus far, will result in further loss of their land and thereby threaten their existence, who can blame them if they do everything in their power to defend their property?"

*Above: Forced labour for the railway construction.
Below: Executed Herero.*

Protest and resistance among Europeans was also caused by the brutal practices of destruction of the colonial troops applied during the German-Namibian War, although only in very few cases did information leak through.

Prisoners of the German colonial regime.

Victim of a German flogging.

One such incident is known which happened on a farm in the South: The farmer and his sons were accused by the German authorities of having lent support to the Nama resisting colonial rule. As a consequence, the sons were sentenced to death in a court-martial and instantly executed on their farm by a firing squad. Their father was brought to Keetmanshoop to face trial there.

Another example of resistance among whites against the colonial practices of the settlers and authorities in Namibia is on record:

Two minor officials in the German colonial office, aware of the misdeeds going on, tried to make them known to their bosses in the office. But their internal reports were just put into files and ignored. The two men insisted that action be taken against these practices. As a consequence, they were forced to quit their jobs in the office because of "mental incapacity". The two then passed on the information to a member of the German parliament who was sympathetic to the Namibians.

This representative showed the documents to the German chancellor and asked for action. But insted, the German chancellor was only worried about the possibility that information had leaked out of the colonial office and ordered disciplinary proceedings to be taken at once against the two officials.

Some old people remember their history:

KING MANDUME OF NORTHERN NAMIBIA

The following report was given by eye-witnesses of the time, some old people from the North. The interview was done in October 1982 at the Health and Education Centre in Nyango. At this time, these old people were more than seventy years of age. They were children when Mandume led the struggle against the British, the Boers and the Portuguese. Among those in the group, one of the women had as a small girl seen King Mandume herself.

The story told refers to the events in 1917, when King Mandume, after several years of successful survival, was finally defeated by the combined efforts of the colonial powers around his territory.

When Mandume heard that the Portuguese were near his place, he organized his people. With a group of them he went to fight against the Portuguese. But except for Mandume and his son, all of the people were killed.

Again, Mandume sent out troops under the leadership of tough and experienced commanders, to fight the Portuguese. But they were also defeated. Upon their return, they had to report to Mandume that the situation was not under control, as the Portuguese were superior in arms. Mandume then decided to retreat and changed the place, but the Portuguese followed him.

When Mandume learnt that the Portuguese were following, he finally decided that it would be better then to fight. Commanding his people, he used some proverbs, saying "This is your motherland, you have to fight for it against those who want to occupy it and take taxes. It is better to fight until we beat the enemy or until we are defeated." So he again organized his people and with his soldiers he went to fight again and won a big military victory against the Portuguese troops.

After this, the British from the Cape sent the Boers to help the Portuguese, and from both sides now colonial troops came to fight Mandume, who faced a severe shortage of ammunition, so he could not last longer.

Mandume told the people that this land is their forefathers land. And he said it in a way that the people understood, that there is no hope any longer in their fight against the invaders. Therefore, during the following night, the people left the place so as not to be killed unnecessarily, as Mandume had indirectly ordered them to do. Only Shikololo, his commander, stayed with Mandume. In the morning of the following day, the

The model of an Ovambo house.

Boers were approaching the house where Mandume stayed. He then called his commander Shikololo, and together they went to a tree nearby. "I think I would better sacrifice myself for my motherland", Mandume told his commander, "and if you have a blade with you, then you can kill me." At first, Shikololo refused to do so. "No, I'm not going to kill you", he said to his chief. Mandume then replied: "Okay, if this is the case, I don't want to be captured by those people. I have fought enough and I want to die as a free man."
So, finally, he killed himself. But before he died, his last words were: "This is our country, our motherland."
And when Shikololo saw that his chief had killed himself, he then killed himself too. that is the story about the death of Mandume.

Tasks:
Oral history and tradition was one of the high cultural abilities our people had. Unfortunately, much of our history has meanwhile been distorted or forgotten through the colonial impact on our daily life. But some people still have much to tell about our past. It is therefore important for us to recall as much as there is still existent in the memory of the people.
— *Gather more stories about our people's history!*
— *Try to reconstruct various historic events by asking older people for information and their knowledge.*

THE OLD NAMIBIAN PEASANT

He is a man of hundred summers
His back bent with age
His corrugated face
Screened the hardship of life

In a small, round hut
Thatched with dry grass and reed
Back in the remotest rural areas
There, he dwells with wife and children

He remembers well - though with pain
The younger days of his life
When he was forced to lead an alien life
And to surrender his labour to the colonialist

He recalls with new freshness
His neck veins glistened with sweat
His black muscular back and
His hands as tough as leather

He held land
He owned cattle
He possessed labour
All was under his control

But as you know sister
Time came and time went
Christianity came and Colonialism followed
And he waited to see

From the Bible in his hand
The missionary preached the "holy message"
And yet with the gun in his pocket
The missionary killed his converts

The chiefs were extorted into treaties
And he, dispossessed of his land, and
His cattle confiscated
Stands here today, exploited and humiliated

He recalls with considerable pride and respect
Hendrik Witbooi
Mandume Ndemufayo and
Hosea Kutako
These were men of courage and resistance

That is what his memory still recalls:
Missionaries' wickedness
Colonisers' cold-bloodedness and
Africans' resistance and bitter sufferings

His face expresses now
A clear significant feature;
"We have offered resistance, and
Our children will carry on the just struggle
Until every inch of our soil is liberated."

Tshuuteni Tshitigona

The Old Namibian Peasant, as the poem is entitled, shows the history of our country from the perspective of an old man. It makes it easy to follow the various stages of our Namibian nation from the personal point of view of individuals. Every one of us experiences history, his or her own life is history, and each one in itself tells part of the story of our people.
— Listen carefully to what the old Namibian peasant has to tell you. He knows from his personal experience.

Tasks:
After reading the poem, you should be able to reconstruct the various stages of our history. List them and discuss each one.
— *Compare the history of the old Namibian peasant with your own experience.*
— *Collect more historic evidence from other old people you know. Compare the personal histories you were able to collect.*

Consequences of defeat:
THE ORIGINS OF APARTHEID

After the German colonial troops had broken the anti-colonial resistance of the Namibian communities by military violence, the administration issued proclamations and laws aiming at the complete destruction of the existing ties among our Namibian people.

One way of doing this — while at the same time it had the effect of improving control — was the systematic establishment of so-called 'tribal reserves' (we've already learnt about this in a previous section on land distribution). The variety of 'tribal reserves' created is shown on the map once more.

These reserves were meant to be an instrument for better control of the Namibian people and for isolating them from each other, to prevent further organisation and, as a result of this, more resistance.

Because the colonial army during the German-Namibian War had killed nearly half of the people living in the southern and central parts of our country, the shortage of cheap labour for the white farms and the expanding mining operations increased. Those Namibians living in the northern areas, mainly the Ovambo, were from this time onward of far more interest to the colonisers than before, as there was a high potential of cheap labour.

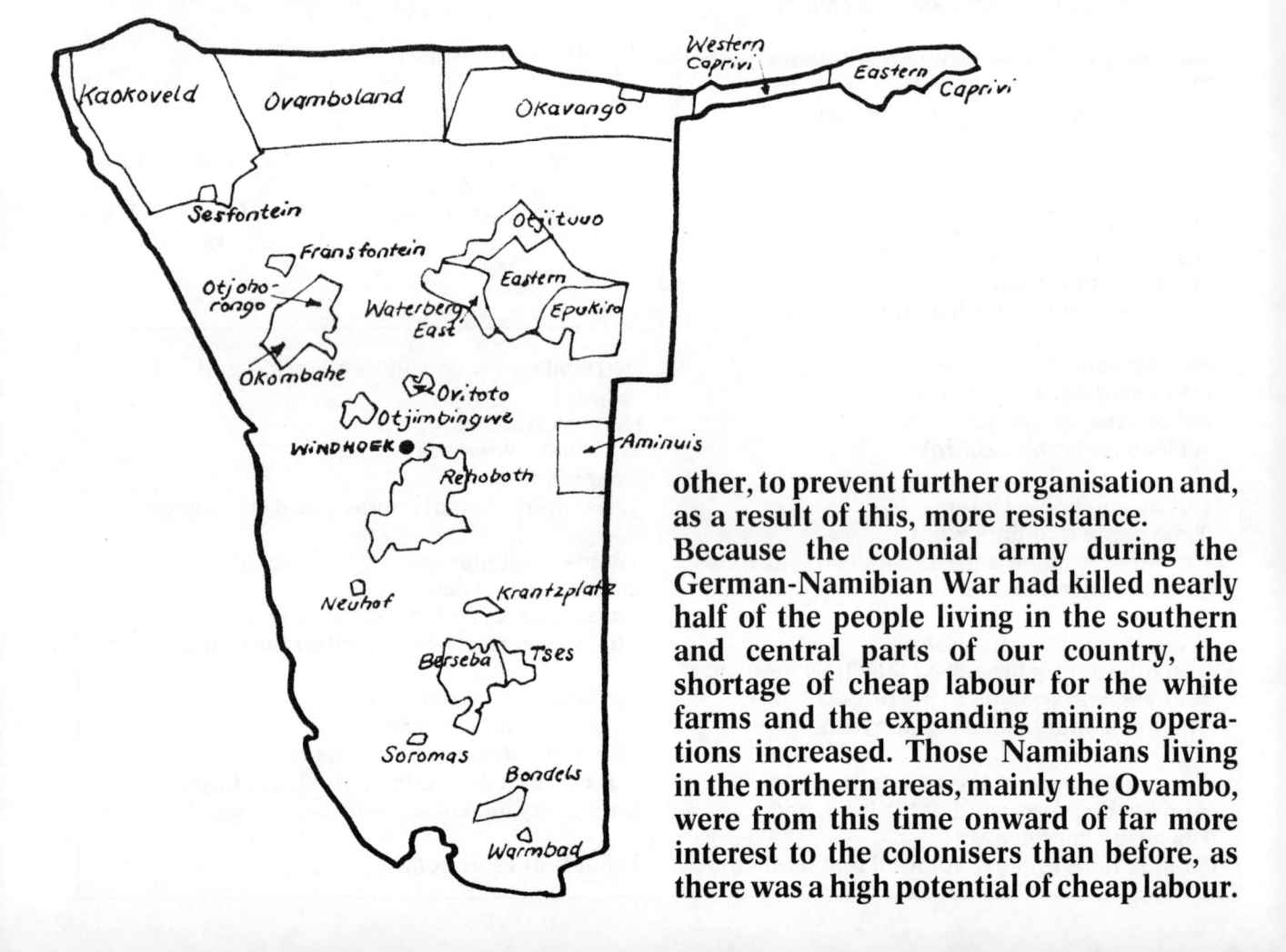

Early this century, therefore, contract labour and migrant work became introduced and established. Recruitment of workers from the north started on an organised scale.

Finally, a third important aspect of the colonial policy emerged: The complete social segregation between the colonisers and the colonised. By means of a number of various regulations the colonial administration prohibited from this time onward among other things, mixed marriages, declared places as exclusively reserved for whites, and introduced pass-laws to control the movement of the people.

The strict segregation along racial lines already established under German colonial rule was a system, which later on became known as the South African policy of apartheid. This means, that in the case of our country Namibia, apartheid was already created before the South Africans took over the administration and simply continued the system.

Scenes from the early diamond-rush: View of a diamond field at Kolmanskop (above right); workers during the search for diamonds (below right); old mining machinery in the Namib near Oranjemund (below).

When World War I started, South African Union troops occupied our territory to fight the Germans. In the course of the short military confrontation, the German soldiers tried in vain to prevent the defeat by destroying parts of the railway line, making it more difficult for the Union troops to move forward (above). The old and the new "masters" (below): After the defeat of the Germans, the South Africa general Botha (right) meets the last governor of former "German South West Africa" and commander of the German troops Seitz.

The change of masters:

SOUTH AFRICAN RULE

When the Germans were forced to leave Namibia, South Africa took over the administration from the League of Nations in the form of a trusteeship. For this, the League of Nations issued, in 1921, regulations for the administration of our country. The most important regulation was laid down in Article 2 of this mandate, saying:

"The Mandatory shall promote to the utmost the material and moral well-being and the social progress of the inhabitants of the territory subject to the present Mandate."

In the beginning, the Namibian people expected that this would change their situation for the better. But instead, the South Africans with their policy simply turned out to be the new occupying colonial power.

The following document shows the disappointment after more than 25 years of South African rule.

Chief Hosea Kutako, leader of the Herero, declared on August 6, 1947, in Windhoek:

"It is the opinion of our people that the lands which were taken away from them by deceit and by force should be returned to them and that they should be enabled to live their life as people. The Herero nation does not wish to dominate any other race or nation. They ask for the right to live their own life as a people. That will require the return of their lands and it will also require the return of the paramount chief, Frederick Maharero, who is now in exile and with him the people who are now living in Bechuanaland together with their cattle.

We do not regard the Union government as fit to be in charge of us as the trustees of African people in this territory. If we are regarded by the Union government as their wards we want the other nations of the world to know that we have been deprived of our lands and we are prevented from developing into a fully grown people by those who claim to be our trustees."

In fact, nothing basically changed for the better for the Namibians under South African rule. Examples following in the subsequent section give ample evidence of this.

Chief Hosea Kutako, Herero leader for more than half a century; died July 1970.

We can learn a lot about the spirit prevailing within the colonial powers during the days of the change of this power in our country by analysing this illustration. It was published as a cartoon in a South African newspaper in 1915 and deals with the defeat of the Germans in Namibia by South African troops in the course of military events of World War I. Typically, our country is just symbolized by a wall, while the Namibian people are not existent at all.

Part III:
OUR NAMIBIAN NATION – SOCIAL EXPERIENCES OF TODAY

Section 5

Evil of the world

Forced resettlement:
– We won't move!
– The old location
– The Windhoek massacre
– Deportation

On contract

Life conditions of contract workers

Namibian contract worker

On strike

Resistance and race

Unity and self-reliance

On colonial mentality

Challenging the system

This poem deals with the same subject of oppression and resistance in a general sense and includes the experiences of all people in the countries of the so-called "Third World".

EVIL OF THE WORLD

Oh, illness of the world,
Evil of the world, evil of the world.
Oh, compatriots, how long? How long?
Suffer'd are you goin' to suffer?

Suffer, not that you want to suffer
But, 'cause of foreign forces
Oh, mama, how long?
For how long, how long, do you think?

Oh, evil of the world,
Poison of the world,
Pollution of the continents,
'cause of your selfishness.

Evil of the world, evil of the world
Source of aggressive wars,
'cause of capital,
Oh, thief of the world.

Oh, freedom-lovers
That's 'cause of him,
That you're sufferin'
Oh, militants, patriots 'n progressives of the world.

Evil of the world, evil of the world.
For how long? For how long?
Will you think of your evils,
Will be allowed, to be the grave-digger
of the world.

Oh, revolutionary force, oh, progressives
It's 'cause of imperialism 'n colonialism,
That you're sufferin' 'n dyin', daily.
Oh, progressives.

Karivazeua K. Hongoze

Tasks:
Read the poem carefully and look at the illustration. Where do you see the common message between text and picture when comparing them? What message is it? Think of some examples for the structure described from your own daily experiences. Try to sort out what everyday features are good examples of what is dealt with in the poem and the illustration.

FORCED RESETTLEMENT

Our Namibian history is filled with experiences of people who were forcefully moved from one place to another. The authorities, following their policies of apartheid and separate development, decided where the black Namibians had to stay and live. Forced to leave their old homes, the people had to move to newly built townships or native reserves declared to be their "traditional homelands".

One important example and experience in this part of our history was the forced resettlement of the people from the Old Location in Windhoek. Until 1960, the black urban population of Windhoek lived inside the city. Then the South African regime wanted to "clean" this area for new buildings of the whites and either sent the people living there into tribal reserves in the countryside or resettled them in a new township outside Windhoek: Katutura. But the people did not want to move and organised broad resistance. They successfully boycotted the resettlement for several years. The text below describes one of the meetings, which frequently took place in the old location during this period, to protest against the forced removal. It is an extract from John Ya Otto's book "Battlefront Namibia" and tells of a public meeting with representatives of the white administration.

The main speaker of the people had already been Sam Nujoma, our President of SWAPO, with John Ya Otto as his interpreter. Read what John Ya Otto recalls from this meeting, which documents the rejection of the system by the people.

"WE WON'T MOVE!"

On the platform we were joined by Chief Kutako and other members of the Herero Chief's Council. I tried to spot familiar faces in the throng. Everybody was here, it seemed: workers in dirty overalls and khakis, clerks in white shirts and loosened ties, women with bright scarves that dotted the crowd with colour, and children running about in front of the stage. They were all restless. ...

Luckily for me, the Boers had brought their own interpreter, a thin Coloured man whom I came to pity more and more as the Native Commissioner, Bruwer Blignaut, began the speeches. Blignaut was trying to be friendly, saying that although it might be difficult for us to comprehend, resettlement in Katutura was really in our interest. He was so out of touch with the crowd before him that they just ignored him, waiting quietly for the next speaker, Superintendent Pieter Andries de Wet, who stepped confidently to the microphone. "We choose the name 'Katutura' because it means 'we want to go and stay there'," de Wet began.

When the thin man translated this opening remark, the crowd suddenly burst into life. "Liar! Liar! You don't even know our language." The people of the Old Location, not the government, had dubbed the new township 'Katutura', meaning 'we are always being moved'. People yelled and shook their fists at the bewildered de Wet. A woman lept on to the edge of the platform. "We'll never move. You'll have to haul our dead bodies to your damned Katutura!" she screamed into the Boer's face. De Wet, who did not understand her words but could not mistake her sentiment, jumped back. Sweat poured off his balding forehead; he was almost swimming in his black suit.

If the officials had more to say, they preferred to wait. After a confused pause, Sam took the microphone. "Is this the best our friends can do?" he began and I translated into Afrikaans. He went on to attack the Boers' reasons for the move to Katutura. Soon the crowd took up the chant, "We won't move! We won't move!" Sam turned to the whites as he waited for the clamour to subside. "Why don't you move," he said when his voice could be heard. "You have shown that you cannot rule us. Go back to South Africa and let us rule ourselves." I was only halfway through the translation when Jaap Snyman, mayor and one of the richest men in Windhoek, leapt from his chair and pushed me away from the microphone. "Don't listen to this communist agitator," he screamed hysterically, "he's leading you astray. We know what's best for you."

A loud, humiliating guffaw rolled through the crowd. Thousands of black people were laughing openly at the mayor to his face. Some began to chant in Afrikaans, "Boers, got to Kakamas! Boers, go to Kakamas!" (Kakamas was a remote outpost in a desolate area of South Africa's Cape Province, and this slogan was soon to become our trademark.) No longer able to make himself heard, Snyman stepped back, his face distorted in frustration, whispered something to his colleagues and, in close formation, the four of them trooped off the stage with the unfortunate interpreter making up the rear. The jeering crowd parted to let them pass. "We'll see who moves," people yelled after them as the Boers' entourage roared off towards Windhoek in a cloud of dust.

Tasks:
In the text, a white official gives his own interpretation of the meaning of the word Katutura, while afterwards its true sense is explained. Discuss, what the word really means and what it stands for. Try to imitate the scenes described by making a play out of it.

THE OLD LOCATION

It was easy to be mistaken about the Old Location. Vast, crowded, the shanty town wrapped itself around the scrubby hills of Windhoek's northern fringe, on the opposite side of the city from the white suburbs. The wiry shrubs gave way to houses made of cardboard, cloth, scraps of plywood, flattened oil drums and other makeshift building materials, thrown together in no apparent order. Only when you got near could you distinguish the shacks, set so close together that some families could easily touch their neighbour's walls from their own windows. Family quarrels behind the thin, gaping walls soon became neighbourhood gossip. Everyone knew one another and strangers did not remain so for long. You knew the streets, unmarked and unnamed, only after you had lived in the Old Location for a long time. Around the irregular rows of shacks, streets snaked and jogged, narrow and dusty. When the rains came, the streets became roaring rivers that washed away shanties and left deep gullies. Neighbours took in the homeless until materials could be salvaged and a new place propped up. Since it was impossible for a stranger to locate anyone without asking, Africans with passbook problems also found refuge from the police there. It was as if the very hardship of life in the Old Location created a great family in which each member looked out for every other.

Tasks:
This text gives you some of the reasons why the people had to resist the resettlement to Katutura. Read it and discuss the motives. Do you understand them? — Try to find people who had been living in the Old Location and ask them for more information.
Those of you who know the situation in Katutura, should tell also about your experiences there. Consult other people who have lived in Katutura and compare these reports with what you have learnt about the Old Location. Try to find out about the basic changes between the two places.
— Consider the change in the meaning of the word SOLIDARITY, when comparing what you know about life in the Old Location and in Katutura.

THE WINDHOEK MASSACRE

The South African regime responded to the resistance of the people with extreme violence. During a peaceful demonstration against the forced resettlement from the Old Location to Katutura, the police opened fire on the unarmed crowd, killing eleven people and wounding many others.
The brutal reaction lead to many discussions on the question of political resistance and armed struggle. The decision of SWAPO to take up arms in the fight for independence has been closely related to the experiences of forceful resettlement to Katutura.
The 10th of December, 1959, the day on which this massacre took place, has been remembered ever since as a cornerstone in the struggle against colonial rule. December 10th is now celebrated annually as Namibian Women's Day, as women were most active among the demonstrators.
A description of the scene after the Windhoek Massacre, taken from John Ya Otto's book "Battlefront Namibia", follows:

The muddy square bore the painful testimony of the previous night's devastation. Pieces of clothing lay scattered about, torn and trampled into the dirt. All the windows and doors of the municipal offices that fronted on the square were shattered. Piles of broken glass along the walls glinted in the early December sunshine. A jumbled heap of blackened sheets of corrugated iron was all that remained of the Old Location beer hall. The fire had cracked open the huge vats of beer and the brown liquid was still oozing into the ashes, emitting a foul steam that settled over the square in the windless morning.
Two municipal workers in overalls were struggling to lift the body of a young woman out of the puddle where it had lain all night. A striped scarf was still wrapped around her head; the upper part of her blue cotton dress was saturated with blood. The water in the puddle was a dark, dirty red.
Four other corpses were already stacked on the truck. As the two workers straightened up with their load, the body of the young woman slipped from their hands and fell rigidly to the ground. The white foreman swore at them from the cab of the truck, but when his eyes met mine he immediately looked away, uncertain, almost fearful. The older of the two workers looked at me and said without force: "Bastards."

Tasks:
Since the resistance to forced resettlement from the Old Location to Katutura and the following Windhoek Massacre were among the important stages of our struggle for independence, you should try to learn as much as possible about this time. Try therefore, to find people who still remember this period from their own experiences and are prepared to tell you about them (possibly, some people who remember well are for emotional reasons not willing or in a position to recall this publicly, which you should then accept and understand without pressing them into giving a report). Try to reconstruct what happened and how much it influenced the further development of our struggle, especially the decision by SWAPO that armed resistance could not be excluded any longer.

DEPORTATION

Many people forcefully removed from their homes in the Old Location were not allowed to stay in the area of Windhoek city any longer. Instead of getting new accomodation in Katutura, they were deported to tribal reserves set up for the various ethnic groups among the Namibian people.

Colin O'Brien Winter, former Bishop of the Anglican Church in Namibia, was expelled from our country by the authorities in 1971. As a white spiritual leader of a mainly black church, he was — like many other whites doing service in the churches — concerned about and devoted to our struggle for human rights. He died abroad, not allowed by the regime to enter Namibia once more. In his book entitled "Namibia", the then Bishop in exile remembers, in the text following, what he observed during his last visit to the Old Location.

On the last occasion that I drove into the Old Location, the final group of Herero were leaving. I watched them sadly as they climbed into the waiting trucks which were piled high with household possessions. Ten families or more could be accomodated in one truck. They had with them a few possessions — the odd chair, a table, a primus stove, a worn mattress. I feld ashamed as I watched the women in their long stately dresses file past me.

The white administration, wishing in victory

to be seen as a benefactor, had sent along a couple of underlings who were to offer the people mealie meal or flour for their journey. Some of the reservations to which they were travelling were hundreds of miles away; poverty and overcrowding awaiting them there. The local press had made much of the fact that the removals were conducted with as much humanity as possible on the part of the white administration.

The two white men stood beside full sacks of mealie meal and flour. I watched the Herero women pass them. Their faces were expressionless; with heads held erect, they glided past the officials who tried to hand to each one a small sack of flour. Not a single woman so much as looked at them or recognized their presence; they were completely ignored.

One little Herero boy held out his hand and accepted a parcel. His mother responded by dragging the child to the side and beating the contents from his hands onto the ground. She then handed her son safely into the arms of her friends who were already seated on the truck.

Tasks:

Some of you might have experienced personally what it means to be resettled by force. And most of you should know what restriction of movement under the pass laws means to a person. Forced resettlement, tribal reserves and pass laws have influenced our society to a tremendous extent. Nearly every Namibian family has been confronted with this system of racial segregation (even the whites, as they were not allowed to enter or move freely in the tribal areas without the permission of the authorities).

— Summarize the experience you or people you know about have had with this system.

— Create some short plays about typical scenes in this system.

— Write a short story about one of your experiences or about what has happened to your family.

— Give reasons why such a system of so-called separate development is not acceptable to an independent Namibia, and why it is an offence to basic human rights.

ON CONTRACT

In this section, we learn about the first experiences of a young Namibian contract-worker from the North nearly 40 years ago. Little changed during the years following. The story is taken from Vinnia Ndadi's book entitled "Breaking Contract":

Recruitment

I was very young - still seventeen in fact - when I first went to SWANLA in 1946. I wanted to continue school, but had instead to think of work. One day I walked to the SWANLA recruiting station at Ondangua. They laughed and sent me back home saying I was too young and weak. Employers buying people from SWANLA wanted strong boys able to do hard work in the mines and farms, not young boys unable to lift even a bag of cement. I was sent back like this four times before they finally accepted me. I really wanted to go.

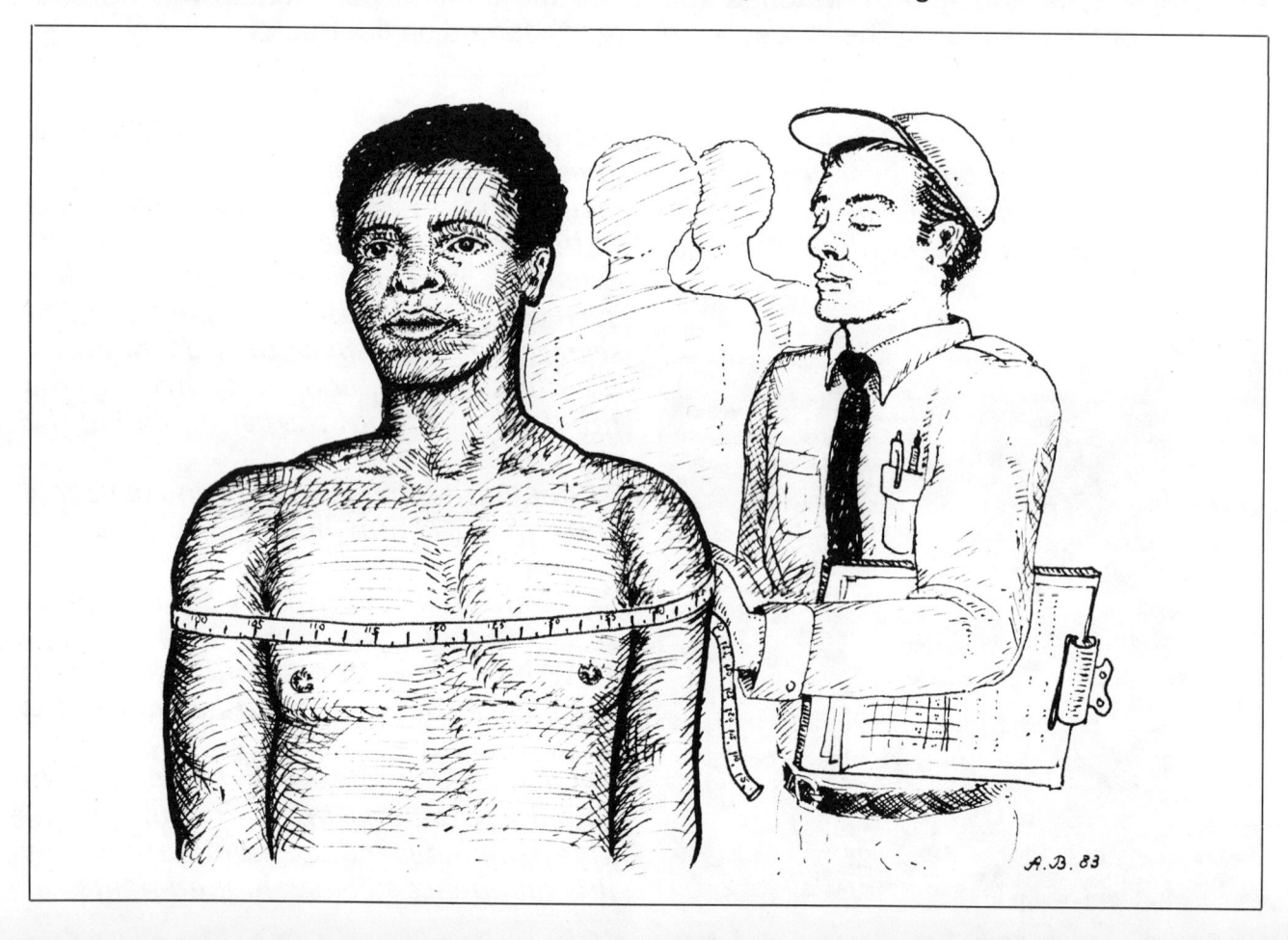

Once accepted I was examined and classified as a "Grade C boy". Workers were classified according to their health; the strength of their bodies. That's the only important thing to the recruiting agent - he doesn't want to buy a sick or weak person unable to perform the work he is contracted for. At Ondangua, after our physical examinations (they treated us just like cattle) they graded the very strong and healthy ones "A boys"; those with good health but not very strong as "B boys"; and the youngest and weakest as "C boys". After my physical examination I was tagged with a number and my "C" classification. I had to wear this tag on a string around my neck.

Later that day all of us who passed were put into buses and taken to the SWANLA camp just outside Grootfontein. As soon as we got there we were formed in a long line while a man counted up the "A", "B" and "C boys". Then we went to the big compound and joined all the others who were waiting for their papers and transport to the south. The camp at Grootfontein consisted of SWANLA offices and barracks for the contract workers, surrounded by a high, barbed wire fence. The workers' barracks were called "pontoks". They had zinc roofs, concrete floors and no beds. Each man just got two dirty lice-infested blankets to sleep on. The place was filthy and hot - with lots of bugs; big ones. The smell was so bad I couldn't sleep for several hours that first night. We had just one bucket for 20 people and I usually preferred to go into the bush to relieve myself. The food was terrible also - just mielie meal and a small piece of meat once a week. They had new recruits mix the dough for the bread with their feet.

Living quarters for a contract worker inside a compound.

The Way South

Finally they assigned you a job: "Johannes! You're going to milk cows on the 'X' Farm"; "Samuel! You'll work at the Tsumeb mines!" And so on. You couldn't refuse. At first I said to myself that I wouldn't just take any job, but when I saw a man badly beaten for refusing his "contract", I decided to take whatever they gave me. Fortunately, I was told, "Vinnia - you'll work as a 'houseboy' for a Mister Jooste. He's a farmer in the Mariental District."

I went by train from Grootfontein to Mariental, in the south. It was a small train that we called "kataula" because it went so fast. We were squeezed into small cattle cars, more than twenty men in each. They put canvas down to cover the cattle mess but it was impossible to lie down. I stood or sat the whole five days to Mariental. There were no buckets or latrines. We just had to wait each time till the next station - if we could - then run to the bush or latrine. Also there was no water at the "kataula"; cattle could survive without it for days. Eating the dry bread from Grootfontein I got extremely thirsty, which was worse than the hunger.

Reception by the Boss

At Mariental station I was told to wait till my boss came for me. I stayed in a station "pontok" till Mister Jooste arrived a week later. He was surprised to find I could speak a little Afrikaans. He said: "Besides being my 'houseboy', you can translate for me with the other workers". Jooste was a very rich Boer with many Ovambos working on his farm. Before we left the station, Jooste went to a hotel in town for something to eat. "Are you hungry?" he asked. "Well, yes baas, a bit", I replied. When we reached some hotel he told a kitchen worker to get me some food. I sat outside and finally the man brought some food and coffee in a tin. I gulped it down immediately. After three weeks on a SWANLA diet I was literally starving.

> **Tasks:**
> *Discuss what you know about contract-labour existing today. As for many other topics, consult some people who themselves have once experienced this thing, i.e. have been employed as contract-workers.*
> *Is there any basic change compared with the first experiences described by Vinnia Ndadi?*

The homes of farm workers ...

... and the garden of a farm.

LIFE-CONDITIONS OF CONTRACT-WORKERS

Following paragraphs describe some impressions of the situation of contract-workers coming from Northern Namibia. It is told from the point of view of a small Namibian boy living for a while with his family in Aus, a town in Southern Namibia. Afterwards, this boy stayed with his uncle near Tsumeb, visiting farm-labourers on contract in this area. The impressions were recalled by John Ya Otto in his book "Battlefront Namibia", and by reading them we learn something about the life the workers on contract have to lead.

Black railway workers' huts near Otjiwarongo.

Far South

Those of the compound people who had no stove in their huts tried to fight off the chill with firebuckets. With coal from the railway they would build a fire in an old pail, which they took inside once the worst of the smoke had blown off. A good firebucket could burn through the night if you got up and stirred it a few times, but it could also be dangerous. Just a couple of doors down from our house, an old worker celebrated one payday with a few too many beers. As his family had been left behind in Ovamboland, there was nobody to wake him when the bucket started to smoke. I happened to be passing by when they carried his body, wrapped in a blanket, out of the cold, dark shack.

The winter was worse still for the shepherds who roamed the mountains above Aus. The slopes provided good grazing for the karakul sheep, whose thick, black wool made fortunes for the German and Boer farmers in southern Namibia. The farmers employed only contract labourers, mainly Ovambos, who had to live with the herds all the year round. With very little food and clothing and no shelter other than what they could build for themselves from rocks and dry shrubs, these shepherds were ill-placed to withstand the icy wind. At times a few of them would come down to visit us - the only Ovambo family in Aus - and thaw their frozen limbs. Bearded and emaciated in their rags, they sat around the kitchen table with Abraham. I heard them talk about friends freezing to death and about beatings by the baas when sheep were missing. But to me their world was far away and their stories were like tales of strange people on faraway continents.

> **Task:**
> *Why, in his story, does the boy experience the contract-labourers, their environment and their stories as strange as tales of people on faraway continents?*
> — Discuss the probable connections between what people experience and what they think.

In Isolation

During my school holidays I often accompanied Isak on his trips to visit farm workers. Our donkey cart was loaded with Bibles and prayer books, which we sold to those of the workers who had money. My job was to give change, write down the names of those whom Isak had baptized and read the verses Isak chose for each sermon. On some farms the men had not seen any African children since they had started their contract - they could never leave the farm - and my presence sparked memories of home and their own families. As I read from the Bible, their eyes would be fixed on me as if I were their own son, mastering the magic of something they never knew. After the service they praised Isak for raising me in this way and brought us the best food they could find. Our visit was like a break in the clouds; they would plead with us to stay longer and to return as soon as we could.

Tasks:
— *How do you feel about the description given above?*
— *Analyse the emotional consequences of contract-labour under the circumstances described!*

— *In these paragraphs, we have learnt about some aspects of being on contract. But what about those family members the men leave behind?*
— *Gather information from women and children about what life without husband or father means and how much his being on contract influences their daily struggle for survival.*
— *Also ask those among you who have experienced a similar situation, separated from members of the family (like being in exile for example).*

NAMIBIAN CONTRACT WORKER

Living in misery and want
Living in deplorable conditions
And poverty
Living in the so-called homeland
Indeed the labourer reservoir

Forced into moving to the capital sector
Forced into leaving the family behind
Forced into abandoning his political affiliations
- hoping to put an end to his sufferings
- Indeed to earn a better living

Deep in the "Police Zone"
No choice of jobs
Swanla dictates instead
In the mining industry
Deep under the ground
Carrying heavy irons

Tsumeb Corporation in charge
Raw materials in abundance
- away to America
- away to Britain
- away to the imperialists

No right going on strike
Working conditions terrible
Living conditions unspeakable
- more and more misery
- more and more sufferings

Geraldt Tjozongoro

ON STRIKE

At the turn of the year 1971/1972, the contract-workers made history: In a nation-wide strike, lasting for several weeks, the whole economy was paralyzed. Through this united action, the Namibian workers gained world-wide attention and drew interest to the conditions they suffer under. And they gave proof of their strength.

The following story is composed of extracts from a report by Shafodino Nehova, who had himself been involved in the national strike. It gives you some insight into the preparations and results of this combined action of Namibian workers, which managed to change Namibia completely, at least for a period of several weeks, and forced whites to do manual labour of a kind they had never done before.

Strikers on the March in Katatura compound, December 1972.

1. Organizing the actions

Soon we began to organize. We would approach one or two workers in each factory, in the railway and building companies. We only talked to those we trusted. All agreed that something had to be done about the contract labour system.

Around that time the South African Commissioner-General for Indigenous People wrote a newspaper article saying the contract workers wanted to work under the system. He said the workers came to the government and asked for jobs, never complaining that the system was inhuman. We used this article to tell our fellow workers: "See, the South Africans are saying that we are pleased with this system, so we should do something to show them that we really don't want it. If we break this system with a strike, we could have the freedom to choose our jobs and move freely around the country; to take our families with us and to visit our friends wherever they are." Everyone supported these ideas.

In the beginning of November we held a meeting on the town soccer field. About six thousand workers from every section of Walvis Bay attended. Chipala Mokaxua, Namolo, Kamati, I and many others addressed the crowd, all saying that we should lay down our tools and go back home. We said the government had no right to interfere with our wages and that we did not need the Labour Association. We also denounced the chiefs for helping the South Africans to organize the system.

The reaction after the speeches was overwhelming and support for the strike swelled. We also voted to send delegates or letters to workers in other parts of Namibia, like Oranjemund, Lüderitz, Windhoek, Grootfontein, Tsumeb and the farming districts to tell them that on December 11 we would go on strike, leave for Ovamboland and tell the chiefs that we would no longer work under the contract system.

Two days before the strike, Kamati, Namolo and I sent a letter to the Commissioner-General of the Indigenous People, the Administrator for Namibia and Prime Minister Vorster explaining our disagreement with the newspaper article the Commissioner-General had written. We told them that they would soon witness our true feelings about the contract labour system. Shortly after, the South African government called a meeting of workers to which the headmen of seven Namibian tribes and Bishop Auala were invited to speak in an attempt to convince them not to strike. But when the headmen took the microphone, they were shouted down. Only Bishop Auala spoke, saying that, in his way, he, too, was trying to change the system.

Someone spoke from the crowd: "Look, our brothers have been arrested and now the white administrators are trying to stop our strike. The Administrator tells us he is considering the matter but wants to talk with the

Bishop Leonard Auala (1908-1983)

Ovamboland authorities first. They are cheating us! All they really want to do is arrest our leaders and continue the system." "All right", he answered, right in the presence of the Special Branch agents who were recording the meeting, "then you have no choice but to go on strike."

The crowd burst into shouting and applause, breaking up the meeting with SWAPO songs. Those who had passes burned them in further protest.

At the same time, the delegates we had sent to Windhoek, Tsumeb, Swakopmund, and elsewhere returned with reports from all over the country that the news had been received with great enthusiasm. The workers in Windhoek and some miners in that area had decided to join the strike immediately. There was great solidarity among the African people. In Walvis Bay, many of those living in the town entered the compound. Even people not working under the contract system came to stay in the compound. Others gave goods to the workers going on strike.

The next day, Monday, December 10th, we informed our bosses that we were leaving for Ovamboland because of our opposition to the contract labour system. Some of the British and American workers supported us. One of them told me: "You must do what you have decided. If you keep quiet and don't do anything, the companies will do nothing to improve your conditions. You must hit them and only then they will change. And if you find some people vacillating, stop them!"

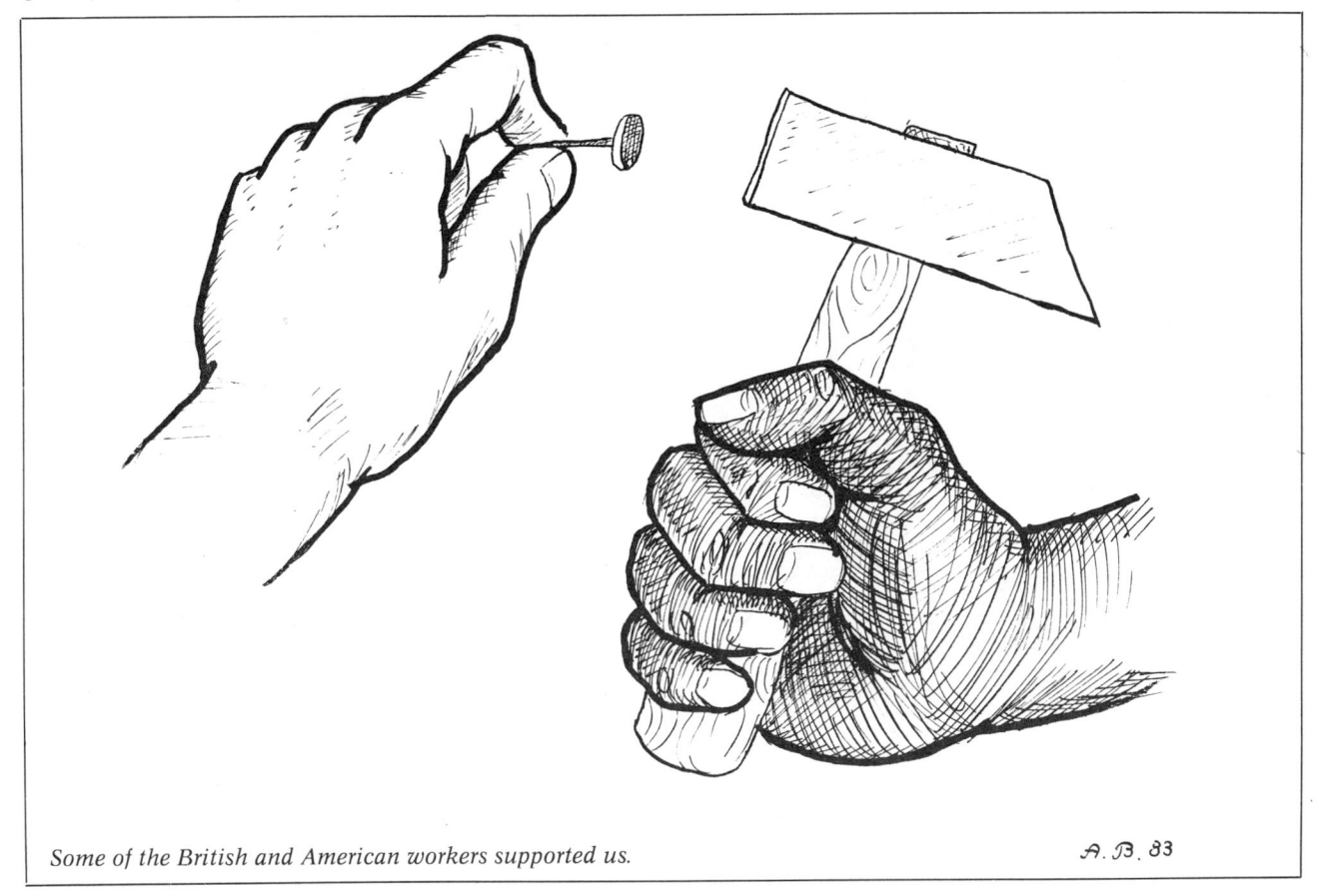

Some of the British and American workers supported us.

2. Boycott, unrest and defeat

The strike began to spread all over the country. The South Africans had made the mistake of announcing it over the radio and this alone had caused a great many workers to leave for Ovamboland. Even small boys working on farms had left their jobs. Within one week, twenty-five industrial centres were hit by the strike. The only place where there were problems was Oranjemund, where the "Baas-Boys", who are paid better than average, had great influence. So only three thousand of the five thousand Oranjemund workers left. But everywhere else, on the farms, in the mines, in the factories, the walk-out was nearly total.

Kamati and I kept in touch with what was going on by listening to the radio and reading newspapers. We couldn't move freely but a number of times we managed to telephone comrades in Ovamboland. They also used to write and keep us up-to-date on developments there. A few days after their arrival, the people were made aware of the strikers demands at a large meeting. The chief and headmen were told that the strike would last until the whole system changed. News of the workers return and the strike's objectives spread across Ovamboland, escalating into many violent acts against the authorities and their collaborators. Many collaborators were beaten and some of the most hated were killed. A great deal of their property was destroyed.

As these activities became widespread, the strikers started more serious actions. For instance, when a headman named Kalengi, who feared reprisals from the people for his collaboration with the South Africans, called the police for protection, they were ambushed by workers with spears and bows. Many people were killed on both sides. We also heard that the strikers had begun to tear down the fence separating Namibia from Angola; in one day five hundred kilometres of fencing between Okavango and the Cunene River was destroyed.

In February, all the headmen in the country met at Oshakati and came out in support of the strikers. This was followed almost immediately by another meeting in Swakopmund which included the Commissioner-General and the Minister for Ovambo Education. The strike leaders in Ovamboland asked permission to take part because changes in the contract system were being discussed but were refused.

We were not represented at all. The South Africans promised many changes in working conditions and salaries, but when the workers returned, the system remained almost exactly the same. Some wages rose slightly but all other changes were simply outweighed by new restrictions and forms of authority.

When the workers saw that things remained basically the same, they started to strike again. However, many of those returning were new, replacing workers who had been arrested. They lacked experienced leadership. Organization among the workers, therefore, was much weaker. Furthermore, the police began to use force: workers were attacked with guns and tear gas. As people were simultaneously being rounded up and jailed in Ovamboland, many of the workers were intimidated. Thus the strike ended in early March.

Tasks:

To go on strike is one of the most efficient ways for workers to articulate their demands and fight for their realization.

— What do you learn from the national strike of 1971/72 as summarized above?
— Discuss the present situation of workers in Namibia under the existing conditions.
— Do you know anything about the situation of workers in different societies?
— What differences can you imagine?
— How should the situation of workers be changed after independence?
— Why do you think it is necessary that workers organize themselves and represent their interests?

RESISTANCE AND RACE

Today, members of SWAPO come from all parts of the Namibian people. Members of the white community have also joined the struggle for national liberation under the leadership of SWAPO, although their number is still very limited. Even in the early years of SWAPO there were whites in Namibia supporting the cause of independence. But according to the circumstances, it was not easy to decide upon the problem of accepting whites within the ranks of SWAPO.

In his life-story, John Ya Otto indicated the problem connected with this issue. The following text is an extract from his book, which is published under the title "Battlefront Namibia".

A few whites tried to distance themselves from the conduct of their brethren. Once, when I was hitching a lift to Windhoek from Otjiwarongo, an Afrikaner family in a station wagon picked me up. I was quiet, as behoves a black stranger, when the man began to talk to me. "Meneer", he said without a trace of sarcasm in his voice, "I know your people will rule this country one day. Today I'm doing you a small favour but tomorrow you may cut my throat."

I was caught by surprise. Did he know I was a SWAPO leader? "No, no", I averred, "I will never kill anybody."

"Please don't misunderstand me", he pressed on. "When the time comes, my family and I will have to pay for what our race has done, even if we don't feel like most of them." He paused and looked at me. "We have created such hatred that people can only see the colour of their skins, not what's in their hearts. I don't blame you; I only know it's true."

This conversation was not the only one of its kind that I had. Despite the increasing violence and polarization tearing at the seams of Namibian society, a minority of whites did try to prevent the total enstrangement of the races. Some even asked to join SWAPO - during 1965 alone I counted more than two hundred such requests. Their initiative caused much discussion in our ranks. It was obvious that not all whites supported apartheid and that there were some who genuinely wanted to work for a democratic, multiracial society. Some were guided by humanitarian views about improving the conditions of our people; others by the simple understanding that the government's present course would lead to bloodshed and destruction. A few of these anti-racist whites we in SWAPO knew well; they assisted us with money, transport, skills and communication with the outside world. Could we exclude people like this from our movement and still claim to be fighting for a multiracial society? Many black Namibians considered every white an enemy but this point of view did not have much support within our organization. Hatred for the whites was an understandable reaction to our life experiences, but it was not an outlook that would promote our struggle. It was becoming clear that just as there were whites who supported SWAPO, so were there blacks - tribal chiefs for instance - who opposed us and would do anything to crush us.

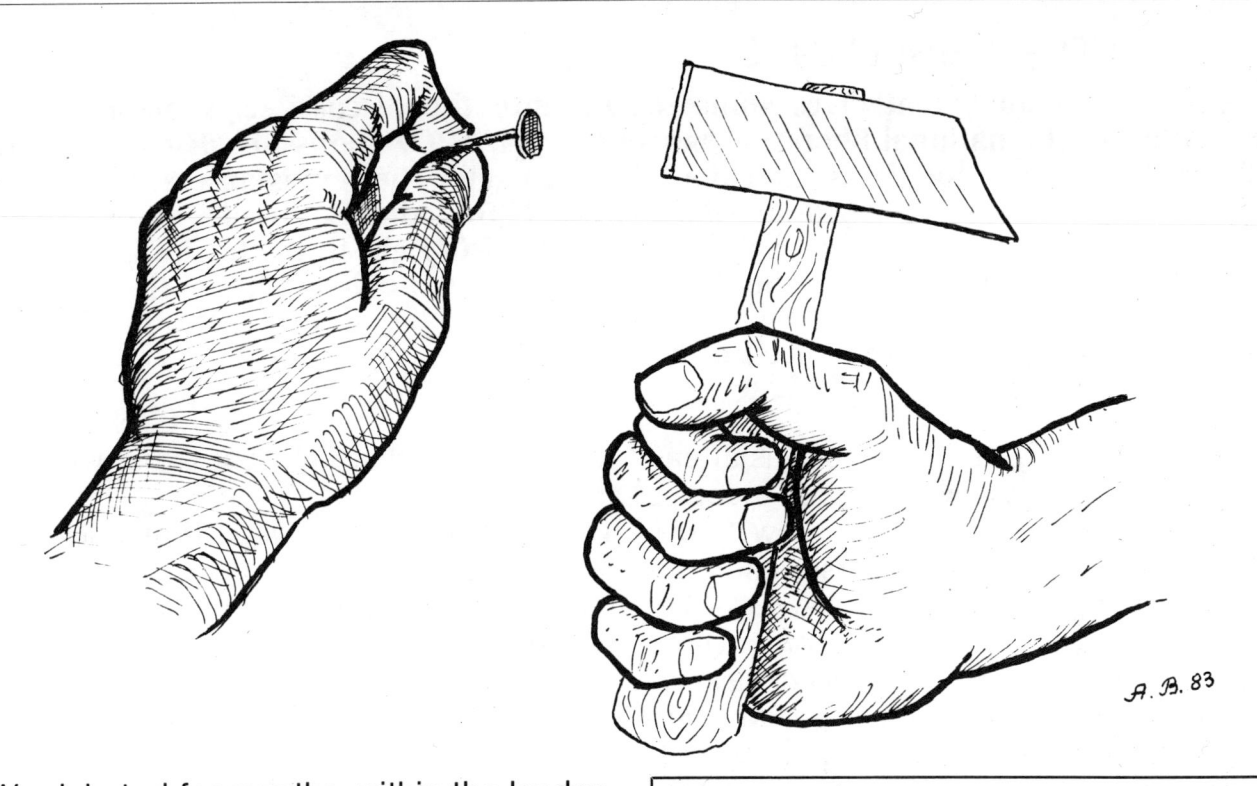

We debated for months, within the leadership and at our membership meetings, before we finally decided that for the time being it would be a mistake to admit white members into SWAPO. There were reasons of security: apart from the handful of well-known friends how could we know which whites to trust? Most of all, however, we weighed the great gulf between the two Namibias: the one in which the many live fenced in, herded about by oppressive laws, exploited to near starvation, and the other in which the few lived in comfortable security, where the conscience sometimes grumbled but never the stomach, and from where it was impossible really to comprehend the things that were driving the many to revolt.

Tasks:
There are several arguments in favour of acceptance of whites and as many arguments opposing admission of whites to the movement.
— *Try to identify the various aspects and discuss them among yourselves.*
— *Why should whites be admitted into the movement?*
— *Why should whites be refused into the movement?*
— *Why is membership of SWAPO as the national liberation movement nowadays open to white Namibians as well?*

UNITY AND SELF-RELIANCE

The following document gives some insight into the discussions soon after the formation of the national liberation movement SWAPO. The issues discussed were of high importance for the further liberation struggle. The text is an extract from a book telling the life story of Vinnia Ndadi, entitled "Breaking Contract". Vinnia Ndadi is one of those fellow-Namibians who joined SWAPO right in the beginning. In his book, he describes his life under South African rule and the first stages of the national liberation struggle. Try to identify and discuss some of the aspects mentioned in the text, which are still of importance for the struggle today.

Our next meeting, at Ohalushu, was attended by more than five hundred people. There were always questions of "How?" How were we going to liberate ourselves? Was the UN going to do it, or SWAPO? One woman asked if the South African government had the right to reject UN decisions. I answered: "The South African government listens to no one. It is strong enough to ignore whoever it likes. They don't even recognize the UN as having legal authority over South West Africa - only the old League of Nations which gave South Africa administrative power in Namibia. The UN knows exactly what is happening here; it has passed many resolutions condemning South Africa, but still nothing has changed. No, we can expect little from the United Nations. Only Namibians can free Namibia!" An old man then wanted to know what kind of a struggle I was talking about - war? "Yes, there is probably no way we can gain our independence except through armed struggle. We must be prepared to fight with anything - guns, bows and arrows, spears... anything! War is a serious conflict. - South Africa must not be allowed to oppress us forever. We must fight back and win our freedom."

The old man's face glowed. "That's all I wanted to know," he said. "You lead, we're prepared to fight. At first I thought you meant only to continue struggling with words. But I agree - it's time we took up guns, spears, pangas!" He said he had fought the Portuguese back in 1917 with King Mandume and the Ukwanyamas. And he still certainly had the same fighting spirit despite his age. I also stressed the need for unity. "Look at the Boers. They have united in order to oppress us, to exploit our labor and our land! If we were to join as one man we could surely defeat them and overcome our difficulties." Kaukungua, continuing on the theme of unity, gave the example of a bunch of sticks. He picked one up. "This single stick you can break easily, but then ten sticks at once? No. It's the same with our struggle: if we are divided the enemy can infiltrate and break us one by one, but if we're together as one strong force determined to get rid of colonialism and oppression, then we will surely win!"

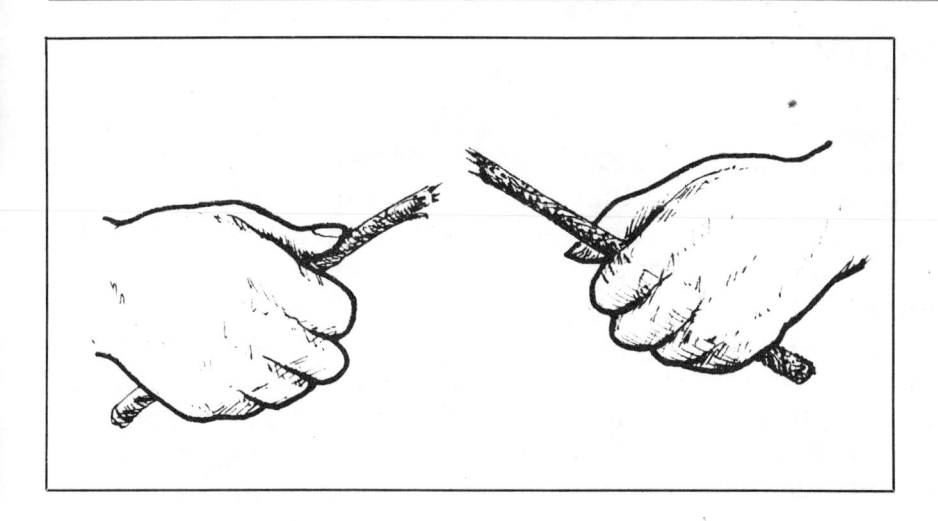

One stick is easy to break...

...but a bundle of sticks is strong enough to resist.

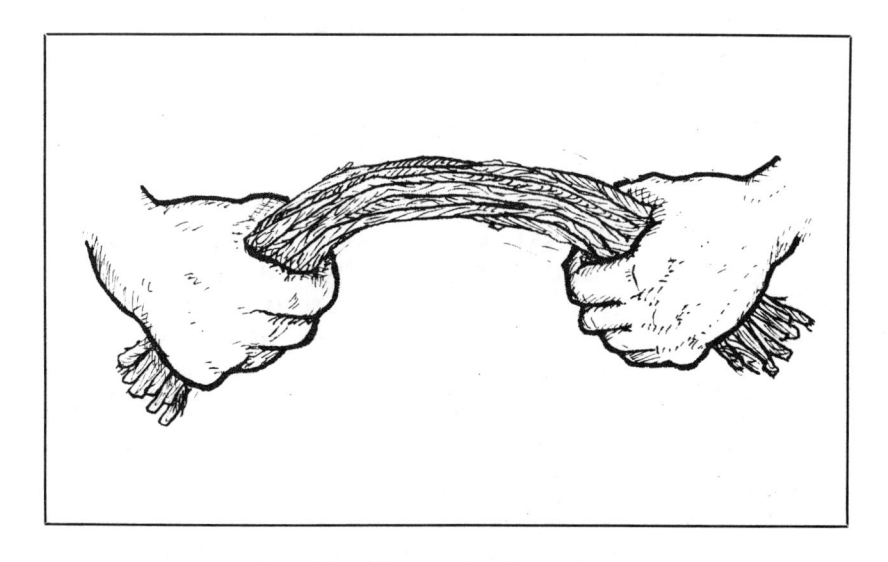

ON COLONIAL MENTALITY

Colonial mentality is something all of us are affected by in different degrees. We all are influenced by colonial mentality as long as our society is organised and dominated along colonial relationships of power. The attitudes and minds of the people reflect more or less openly the influences of our colonised society and its structures. - Even after independence the colonial mentality will exist further and has to be attacked by ourselves.

There are many examples in all areas of daily life that show the deep influences (on our minds too), resulting from more than a century of the colonial system in our country. We take one typical example from a report about the life and the behaviour of black workers in a Namibian mine compound of the Tsumeb Corporation. It shows how the communication between people of black and white origin in Namibia has been influenced by the power of the whites and the struggle for survival by the blacks, who adapt to the conditions by imitating what they think is expected from them. The black worker, by showing servitude and the characteristics the white woman is expecting, tries to gain little privileges and benefits, while the white woman in this true story in return extends them to him for his subordinate behaviour, which confirms what she expects from black Namibians.

In the following paragraph, the black worker tells you how he managed to get some old clothes from a white woman:

I spoke nicely: "Missus, I the old boss's clothes get." (Note the use of broken language.) Add a smile and look humble. She may say: "You have money. For what are you going to use the money?" But, you reply that you are poor and have no money. You must smile or she will chase you away. By smiling she will see friendly intentions and be put at ease. If you do not smile, she may think you are demanding in an uncivilized way as if you are demanding your own thing. If she calls you 'Kaffir', it is not important. What is important is getting the clothes.

Will she not laugh at you if you say you are poor? No, if you say you are poor, then she may help you willingly. If you are keeping to yourself as if you don't mind, then she will refuse because you are proud.

You see the notion is that you are a Kaffir, somebody with a low standard of life as compared to that of Whites. You know there are some Whites who do not want Blacks to improve their living conditions and some will not appreciate it very much if you come to them with a proud attitude. Such people will simply chase you away. You must show that she is a superior on whom you rely for assistance. You must make her feel you are somebody poor who is only relying on her assistance and cooperation. Do not show independence - you may be in for trouble. You must not show that you are clever or educated. She will hate you.

Tasks:
— Imitate the scene described above within your class.
— Change roles and construct similar examples.
— Do you know some from your own experience? Try to remember and arrange them as little plays.
— Discuss with your classmates the meanings of the various scenes performed and the motives and expectations behind the characters behaviour and interaction.
— Write down characteristics and attributes which in your opinion are typical for what could be called a 'colonial mentality'.
— Where do you think you have attitudes which would still fall under this category?
— Also take into consideration subservient behaviour in all spheres of life (e.g. also in the classroom).
— Make a list and discuss the features collected and described.
— Suggest how to combat such attitudes.

The saying "Old attitudes die hard" appears in the Political Programme of the national movement SWAPO. But in a free and independent society all Namibians, regardless of colour, origin, sex and social position should develop consciousness of self and personal pride. This allows communication with each other free from patterns of behaviour based on dominance and servitude. We have to believe in ourselves, in our personal ambitions and achievements, and in human rights based on equality with others.

Tasks:
— *Construct personal interactions, in which various people with different backgrounds communicate with one another on à level of equality and partnership. Select examples from the following fields of interaction (and if possible, add a few more typical relationships):*
— *husbands and wives;*
— *employers and workers;*
— *parents and children;*
— *teachers and students.*
— *Discuss the different ways in which decolonised relations might affect each of the fields of interaction, and the implications this has. After doing this, re-perform the plays you acted out, on the basis of the insights you gained in the discussion.*

CHALLENGING THE SYSTEM

The following document describes one example of collective resistance to the oppressive system. It took place at a time just after OPO, the forerunner of SWAPO, had dissolved and mobilised for the newly found national liberation movement. Nathaniel Maxuilili, one of the SWAPO-leaders, was in charge of this political rally in Walvis Bay. As the event demonstrates, an united and collective action is sometimes even able to challenge, in certain situations, those in power. It is the strength of the powerless, which we could take as a lesson from this topic.

Several thousand people had gathered when four police jeeps suddenly appeared from out of the fog. Wheels spinning in the sand, the jeeps roared straight through the crowd to our truck and unloaded about twenty policemen armed with automatic rifles. They formed a line and moved slowly towards the crowd.

The people at the front backed away and some of those on the fringes were already retreating into the fog, towards the African location. But Maxuilili had other ideas. He grabbed the megaphone. "Everybody stay where you are!" he commanded. "There is no need to leave. This is a SWAPO meeting; we did not invite the police. They are the ones who will have to leave." Maxuilili aimed his megaphone down at the uniformed whites. "And I mean now!"

The policemen looked at each other, dumbfounded, but kept their rifles still. ...
"Policemen, this is a SWAPO meeting. Move your jeeps out of the way. If you want to listen to our speeches, stand back." ..."We give you three minutes."

Three minutes and then what? The plainclothes officer in charge of the troop looked blankly up at Maxuilili, who gave the Boer a burning evil stare in reply. ...Maybe he knew the police mind well enough to play this dangerous game, but I felt weak in my knees as I glanced at my own watch: one minute had passed, and no one had moved. Most of the crowd had stayed on, and now they cautiously began returning for a better view of the showdown, forming a tight throng around the twenty policemen. The officer called his sergeants over for a whispered consultation. They looked out over the silent crowd, shook their heads, glanced over their shoulders at Maxuilili who glowered back at them. ...Two minutes.

As the discussion among the officers continued, a rumble of voices rose in the crowd of people around them. Walvis Bay had been an OPO stronghold from the beginning and the cannery workers had staged several strikes, the latest in 1959 when all the canneries had been forced to close. To the people in this crowd, confrontation with the police was nothing new.

"You have thirty seconds," Maxuilili's stern voice came through the megaphone. The crowd grew louder.

The police sergeants dispersed quickly, waving their men back into their vehicles. In silent disbelief, the crowd parted to let them through. A few moments later, the last jeep had disappeared over the dunes.

"Africa!" Maxuilili shouted.

"Africa!" the people roared.

"Where are they going?" he asked, pointing into the fog that had swallowed up the policemen.

"Kakamas!" the crowd screamed.

"And what will we have?"

"Independence!"

"Those who want to be ruled by the Boers, raise your hand."

Thunderous laughter. Our meeting had started.

Tasks:
— *Dramatize this event!*
— *Try to remember other occasions of either individual or collective resistance challenging the system.*
— *Dramatize such events!*

Part III:
OUR NAMIBIAN NATION – SOCIAL EXPERIENCES OF TODAY

Section 6

My mother

Leaving home

Cecilia Nabot – Profile of a Namibian woman

Exile

The story of Theresa

The strength of women

Kassinga

Learning for the future:
– Our school
– Our new school
– In the holidays

When shall I go

MY MOTHER...

Oh! my Mother, how long shall we bear this?
How long shall we suffer like this
In the country of our birth?
How long my Mother...?

It was yesterday you told me that they have taken my Father
It was today you have told me that they
have taken my Brother too,
Who will be tomorrow,
Oh! my mother how long...?

You told me that they have taken my father
Just because he was a member of SWAPO
You also told me that they have taken my brother
Just because he was at a SWAPO meeting
Where are they? my mother
Where have they gone? My mother
When will they come back to us? my mother
Oh! my mother how long...

Mbunga wa Hoveka

Tasks:
The poem above, written by a student of the United Nations Institute for Namibia while in Lusaka for training, expresses the grievances and sorrows of a black Namibian under the repressive South African system in Namibia.
Many of you have experienced this repression and have suffered under the same conditions. Some others might have been lucky enough not to share these experiences, but it is important for them to get an insight into this sphere, as it influences people for a life-time.
— *Think how these experiences have influenced you personally and try to find out how important they were for your own way forward.*
— *Share your experiences with the others, especially those who haven't had to be confronted with them.*
— *Also, discuss whether political repression in occupied Namibia creates any difference between black and white opponents to the system.*

LEAVING HOME

There follow three personal accounts, in which some of our young fellow-Namibians describe how they left Namibia. They wrote about their experiences on the way into exile. Some of you should be able to tell about similar experiences, the others might be interested to learn about them.

Tasks:
Read the stories carefully. Those of you who have had similar experiences, should try to tell the others about them. Those who stayed at home should try to imagine what such a decision means.
Some of you might have thought about the possibility of doing the same, but came to the conclusion not to leave. There are good reasons for such a decision, and you should explain them.
Maybe some brothers and sisters close to you have once decided to leave, and you have then experienced the feeling of being left behind. Explain to the others what it meant to you and the other members of the family.
Ask those who have taken such a decision to move into exile about their motives and experiences.

It was on the 14th of May, 1980. I thought the whole day how I could cross the Namibian-Angolan border.

I was not alone on the way, but I was with combatants of the South West African People's Organisation. They told me what I should do if we met the enemy soldiers. The journey was long and we did not sleep the whole night. We didn't have anything to eat or to drink with us.

When we were approaching the border, the combatants told me to take off my shoes, because the shoesteps made a lot of noise. When we had crossed the border area, I could put on my shoes again. We did not meet the enemy, but I was very tired.

In Angola I found many combatants. They gave me food and anything else I needed. They told me that I had now become a member of SWAPO. Those combatants who brought me to Angola were not there any longer. They had gone back inside the country.

The next day I was taken by car to Lubango, where I met many other people from Namibia. Some of them were my classmates back home. In Lubango I visited the Education Centre.

Now I am in Kwanza Sul in the Education Centre. Here I am continuing my classes, because to study hard is also a part of our struggle. I do this for my people and for our beloved country Namibia.

Ndategako

On the 18th of March, 1980, I decided that I had to cross the Angolan border. The same day I met two girls and asked them if they wanted to come with me and cross the border as well. They told me that they wanted to do the same.

The day afterwards I met the soldiers of our movement SWAPO. I asked them when they were going back to Angola. They answered that they were leaving in two days. I asked them if they would take us along, and they agreed.

I informed them that we were three persons and they asked me not to add more to the group, because sometimes they met with our enemy, the South African soldiers. Two days later we took our things and started on our journey.

On our way we met South Africans near the border-fence. One of our SWAPO-soldiers saw the army-truck of the enemy, and the racists almost saw us. Then we crossed the border without any danger. I was very happy. I will never forget that day.

Taimi

It was wonderful the day I crossed the Angolan-Namibian border. It was on the 1st of December 1980. First I left my home and went to another village. There I stayed, because I did not see combatants to take me along. Then I left that village and went to another one. But before I arrived, I saw a big group of people in front of me. First I was afraid of them. But two of them came to me and asked, whether I would like to go with them, so I joined the group.
We went the whole night. Before we came to the border we made two lines. Each line of people had combatants in front and at the back. After we had passed the border, we were finally in Angola. I then came to Lubango, and in the camp I was asked about my age. Then I was sent to the Education Centre and from then on I have been attending school.

Martha

A personal history:

Cecilia Nabot – Profile of a Namibian woman

The following story gives an example of how the life of a person is influenced by the political and social circumstances around him or her. This biographical note was compiled in June 1982 by the Namibia Education Centre in Kwanza Sul.

1. Resistance and repression at home

Cecilia Nabot is a married woman. Her husband is the headman of the village Olupale, situated in the North-Eastern part of Namibia. But differences of political nature arose when the husband started to collaborate with the South African authorities. He spied on his wife as well as on other SWAPO activists. After all, Cecilia Nabot not only assisted in the burning of the veterinary offices during the national strike of 1971/72, but indeed had been the one who set fire to that veterinary office of Olupale village with the assistance of two boys.

Soon after this incident, the husband accompanied the South African soldiers to Olupale village and assisted them in their investigation and interrogations. His wife Cecilia was also interrogated, but kept her strength by not admitting to any wrong doing. On that very day, the husband called her a very dangerous underground snake.

In the absence of her husband, the South African soldiers came back. Luckily, on this day, only one black soldier was present. He warned Cecilia in the vernacular not to admit that she was Cecilia Nabot, whose name, age and number of children appeared on the paper the soldiers were carrying. Confirmation of this could surely have cost her life. Instead, she told them that she was a sister to her husband and was just there to take care of the children, while the parents were away. After telling this to the white South African soldiers, Cecilia was released.

2. Assistance to a fighter

Three years after this incident, a SWAPO fighter who had been captured and tortured by the South African soldiers, by chance crawled into her house. He had just been released from Rundu jail, where he was dropped on the banks of the Kavango river. The comrade was dead-tired and very weak, since he had spent many days without any food. Without hesitation, Cecilia and one of her sons took care of the comrade for several days.

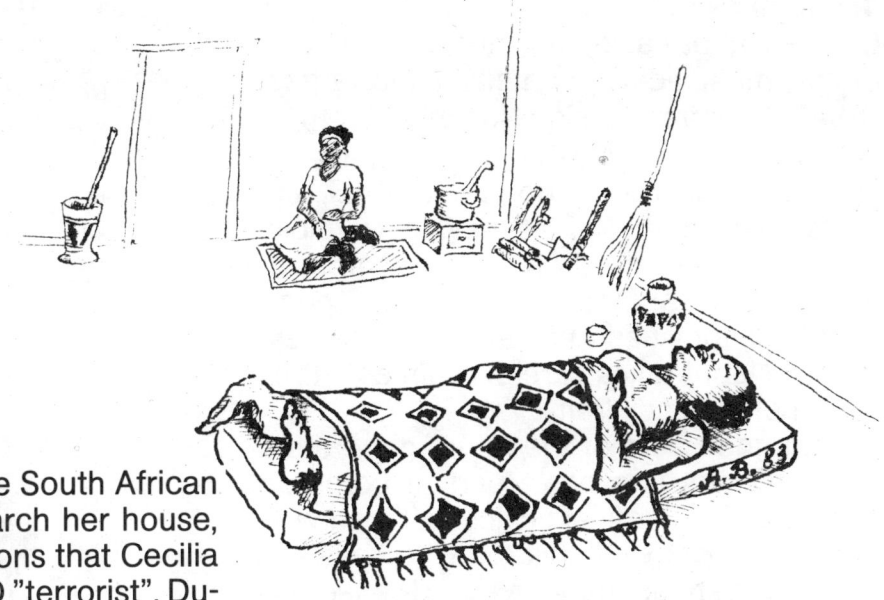

During this time, there came South African soldiers who wanted to search her house, because they had informations that Cecilia was taking care of a SWAPO "terrorist". During the interrogation, Cecilia denied any knowledge about the "terrorist".
But when she was released to return to her home, she saw nothing left apart from the smoke of her house. In her absence, all her property was burnt down by the soldiers. At this point, she took the final decision to leave Namibia. With all her children she crossed the Northern Namibian border area into Angola, where she and her children were safe.

3. Life in exile

Cecilia Nabot has meanwhile become one of the most active women in the largest SWAPO centres outside Namibia. Her main responsibility lies with the young generation, especially for those who had left their parents back home when leaving Namibia. Some of these children were not able to reach the SWAPO refugee centres in good health, as they had to make a long journey. Cecilia Nabot takes care of them as if they were her own children.

Taking good care of the future generation of Namibians is a basic part of comrade Cecilia's life. Her final advice to those who intend to work with children who have endured sufferings, hunger and diseases, is that they must have a sound and deep love for children and an interest in people. They must be dedicated to the future of their nation and, above all, these adults must have self-discipline and self-control.

For Cecilia Nabot, taking care of children is the essence of being a responsible adult. This is her unique contribution to the Namibian struggle for national independence.

Tasks:

There are many people with similar or different experiences. You certainly know some of them.

— *Take one of such people you know as an example, and write a biographical note about him or her by yourself.*

— *Finally, as each and every individual has a history of his or her own, you are yourself a person with specific experiences. Therefore, you can also write down your personal history. This personal history of each and every Namibian is part of the history of our Namibian nation.*

EXILE

The poem following has been published in an issue of Omahungi Vehi, a church magazine for black Namibians. It was written by a fellow Namibian and expresses the yearnings of so many thousands of us who are exiles:

Shall we meet again at home
To talk and sing again
To walk and sit again
In our homes?

Shall we meet at home -
What a meeting it shall be.
Shall we meet again
in the land of our love?
In the land of our dear hope?

Shall we meet again at home
And end the longing of home
And send the wronging home
And from sorrow ever be free?

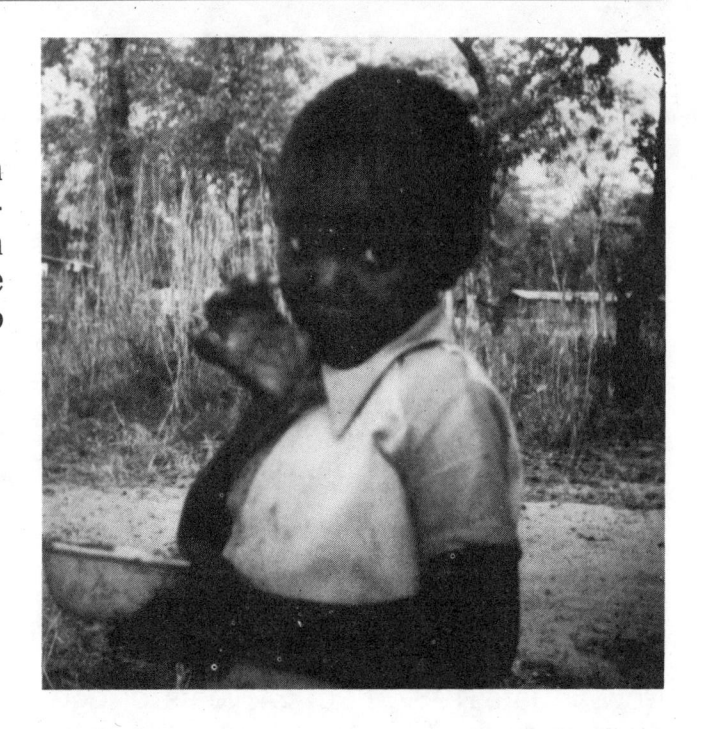

Children at Nyango

Tasks:
— *Those of you have experienced exile yourselves should also try to express your feelings. Those never forced to go abroad should try to imagine what it means.*

— *Remaining at home can also mean to take a conscious decision. Those of you who have decided to stay, in spite of the pressure, should describe the reasons for this courageous position.*

THE STORY OF THERESA

On the following pages, we learn more about the experiences of the generation of young Namibians involved in the struggle for liberation of our country. One example out of many is Theresa, a student coming originally from the Southern part of Namibia. The story she has to tell about her individual development is representative for many other fellow-Namibians. We should therefore listen carefully to what she has to say. It allows us to follow a path many young Namibians have decided to walk.

Part I:
The struggle at home

Theresa in October 1982.

Now, in late 1982, I am 24 years of age. I was born in 1958. My parents are living in Gibeon District. From 1973 until 1976 I went to Tses secondary school. During that time I was involved in the demonstrations taking place at that school. They started after the Soweto riots in mid-1976, when the Boers imposed Afrikaans upon the schools in South Africa.

The Soweto students sent a message to us, and asked us to organise some support in solidarity with their protest and struggle. So around May or June 1976 we were discussing the issue as we were basically facing the same situation, although we already had Afrikaans being taught at our schools in Namibia. But our struggle is the same thing. Therefore we decided to go along with them, and that we would be demonstrating just to show that we live under the same system. We, the matriculants, were the first ones during this time to sit for exams, and we decided that we were going to tear up the papers for these exams. It was also decided that the others following us were going to do the same thing.

In the morning we came to the examination hall, but something must have leaked out about our planned action. The authorities must have been informed. The inspector was coming. This inspector, of course, was a white guy, a Boer. He held a long speech telling us about the importance of matric and what doors a successful matriculation examination would open for us. All that stuff.

After the inspector's long speech and a prayer we started with our action. It was organised in such a way that the matriculants were demonstrating inside the room, while the others from standard 6 to 9 were demonstrating outside the room we were sitting in. And when the inspector was praying with us, those outside were shouting black slogans with raised fists. And after this prayer we were just standing up and shouting "SOWETO!", and tore up our papers. The inspector then became afraid of us and immediately left the room, because he thought that he could be attacked. But not one of us had anything like this in mind.

As the secondary school in Tses is not a government school, but a church school, we had already decided beforehand that we would not damage anything. So he could leave with his car, and even his car was not damaged by us. Otherwise the church would have been asked to repay the damages, and we wanted to show that we were protesting against the government system and not against the church school.

When we had finished our action we left the classroom, went back to our rooms and then a meeting was called at which we discussed the events. We decided not to go back to school and not to sit for any exams. And even the students of standard 6 and 8 decided the same and also destroyed their papers.

Then we appointed three people who should try to keep contact with everybody after all of us had left school and gone home. The students at the school came from down south as far as Upington. I don't think there were people coming right from the north, but there were people from Walvisbay and towns like Karibib. I think this indicates approximately how far the region stretched from where the students at the school were coming. So it was important that each and everybody tried to keep contact with each other.

At the same time as we had our meeting, there was also a discussion going on among and with the teachers, who were on strike as well. I think this had something to do with the salaries. They were in Gibeon. So we sent some people there to find out what had been happening. And finally the whole actions turned out to be something against the wrong system in operation, and teachers and students were expressing their feelings and resistance together against this system. Everyone of us departed and went back home. And that was it. Afterwards, a couple of priests working at the school in Tses asked the South African government officials not to do anything with any of the students, as they as priests at the school did not consider anything in the actions to be illegal. But the South Africans tried to round up the people, even though they could not do anything as long as the church tried to back them.

After some time, they also came to Gibeon to look for me. At that time I was together with a friend from the same class. Firstly, they were looking for him. They wanted to know from us who was involved in the actions. After they interrogated me for quite a time, they brought me back home to my parents.

After this, of course, we did not return to school any more. My parents had problems accepting this. One of the reasons was that they still believed in the value of school education, and, of course, they expected me to complete my education. But then I told them what had happened and what the whole system is about. "You see", I said to them, "even if I succeed and complete my education, the doors will still not be open. I won't be able to go around and find the job I would like to do, or even get a fair salary for what I am doing." And I told them that for all these reasons I wasn't going back to school.

Tasks:
After reading this first part of Theresa's story, you should know why she and her classmates refused to continue their education and why they even boycotted their final exams. Theresa also had to defend this decision against her parents, whose belief in education was still strong. This shows among other things the problem of different generations and their different values according to age.
Take up the topics of education, parents and political values. Discuss, under which circumstances you think it could be justified to disagree with the parents, and whether education as such is undisputable. If you have any, recall your own experiences under the South African educational system and compare it with the training you are receiving now. Tell the others about your experiences.

Part II:
Departure from home

Since I had decided that I wasn't going back to school, and at the same time knew that I wanted to contribute to change in Namibia, I decided to come out and join the comrades outside. That was the major reason why I left Namibia, for the independence of our country. Although there was so much propaganda from the Boers, such as telling us the people outside were suffering. They pretended to know that our people didn't have food, clothes and things like that. And we even had to pray in church for them. But I decided that I would have to go and join them to fight with them for the independence of our country.

I talked to my parents, but they couldn't accept it. Of course, no parents want their children to leave them. But I told them that my mind was going to be changed. And it would have been the same thing whether

I was with them inside Namibia or whether I was in exile. If I were staying with them, and the South Africans come to pick me up, they would also not see me any longer. So they can't say, if I stayed with them in Namibia I would be with them. Therefore, it would be even better if I were outside, because at least I would be free then. And I would be able to fight. While in Namibia in jail I couldn't do anything. And that was the way I convinced them. But I didn't tell them when I was going. I just told them that I was planning to go.

Then, in December 1976, I left Gibeon and went to Windhoek. There I stayed with my brother. Having just left my parents, I felt rather bad. My mother was very sick at this time. She had heart problems and she was really feeling weak. And as she is old already, I didn't know whether I was going to see her once more. I did not even expect her to live on for such a long time, but at the moment she is still alive. But although she had been in a really bad state of health at that time, I had to leave. I knew that this would be one sacrifice I had to make for a better future for Namibia. This sacrifice I also had to make for my own family, my brothers and sisters. Altogether there are eight people in my family. There are only two of us girls out of six children, and I am the second youngest child in the family. Presently in our family there are two of us abroad. One of my brothers is now in Angola. The rest are still at home.

Tasks:

This second part of Theresa's story gives insight into the problems with such a decision to leave home and to leave behind the parents and other members of the family.

Among those of you reading this story, many have certainly experienced similar situations. You had reasons for your individual decisions and were confronted with friends and relatives who either accepted or refused to accept these reasons. To be separated from those close to oneself is often painful. But in many cases it is better to accept this than stay at home.

Discuss this issue in the class and exchange reasons for the one or the other decision. Be careful not to blame anybody for his arguments too quickly, as this question is a very difficult one to answer. It has much to do with personal feelings and emotions and cannot be solved on an abstract and general level. Instead, you should discuss this topic mainly to gain knowledge about the various motives people have. Also try to consult parents or other persons representing a different point of view in order to understand their position, too.

Part III:
Experiences abroad

From Windhoek I finally left for Botswana. I didn't go alone, but we were a group of ten students. The students in our group came from various schools all over the country. Besides us, other students had also left or were going to leave. During this time in December 1976 we were altogether 56 students who left Namibia. We were from all the high schools. We left in small groups and then met again in Botswana. Each of our group had 10 to 15 people. There was no problem with transport or anything else, as we could make use of a good organisational structure. Even when we met in Windhoek, we already had transport available.

We left Namibia via Gobabis. Of course we had to be careful, because the South Africans were watching the border. But since there are farms around Gobabis, we could pretend to visit people on one of these farms. And I think they were not watching the border area very carefully. I think they are also human beings, and that some of them are sleeping most of the time.

When we got to Botswana, we went to the border post there. Then we told the police where we came from and who we were. They kept us there for one day. They were not very surprised. They knew about the situation in Namibia and they were very kind to us. They helped us with food and everything. The next day the Botswana government gave us transport. They brought us first to Ghanzi and then to a camp in Maun. The Red Cross were taking care of us, and we had our own tents.

I stayed there in Maun for one and a half months, and then I went on to Zambia. I went directly to Lusaka. But the few of us who went to Lusaka did not stay there for long. We were just there to fill in our applications for passports. Then from there we went down to the places where our camps were. I went to Senanga. That was in early 1977.

When I went to Senanga, I first received some training as a nurse. This was very good experience, especially for working as a nurse afterwards in one of the SWAPO camps. And then a group of ten were chosen to go on and study medicine. I was in this group, and that was the reason why I then went to Nyango. I left Senanga in May 1978. When I was in Nyango, I was working in the hospital, and then started to work at the school as a teacher there. I was teaching for six months and then, finally, I came to Lusaka to take up my studies at the University of Zambia. That was in November 1978.

My studies are paid for by the World Health Organisation. But it turned out to be a big problem in the beginning, that I had not finished school at home and did not have the matric. When I started my studies at the University of Zambia, I could not present any qualifications to study in the field of natural sciences. And my knowledge of history also turned out to be very weak. This was a result of the vague and distorted history courses at home. I did not know anything about Africa as such, but only about the South African perspective of the white history. In the field of natural sciences, I had only had biology in school, but no physics and no chemistry.

It was important that the people in Zambia also understood the situation and the problem. They therefore offered me a chance by letting me enrol for the first term. If I didn't succeed during the first term, I would have to leave. But during the term they felt that we were trying to do our best. So we passed this test year. But I really had to work hard.

There was one lecturer who was British, but who had also taught for five years in South Africa. From that time he knew about the situation there and also did not like it. He helped us very much in our efforts during this test year and even tried to explain things to us in Afrikaans. But nevertheless, it was a very tough time.

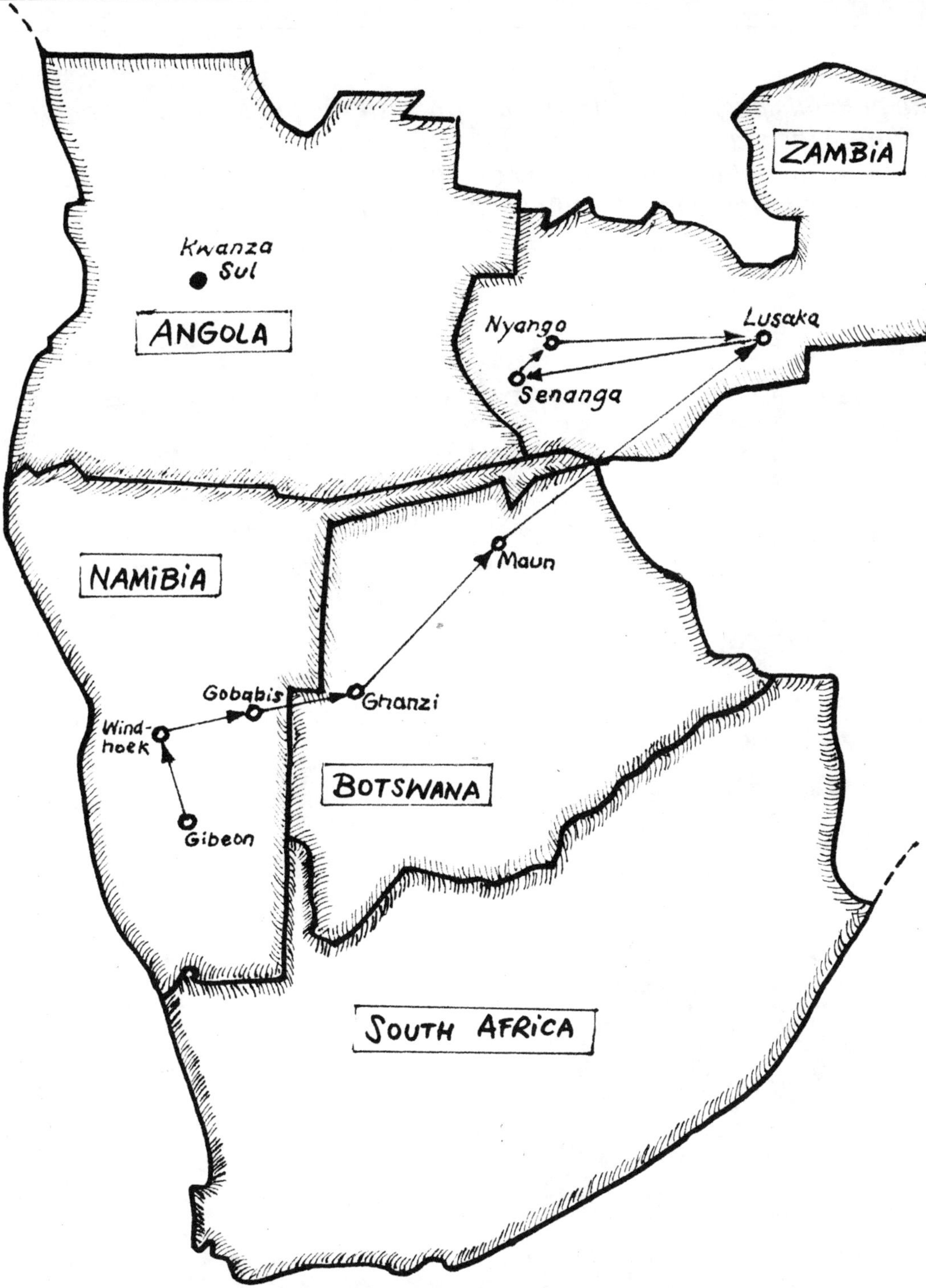
ZAMBIA
Kwanza Sul
ANGOLA
Nyango
Lusaka
Senanga
NAMIBIA
Maun
Gobabis
Ghanzi
Wind-
hoek
BOTSWANA
Gibeon
SOUTH AFRICA

Tasks:
On the previous page, you will find a map with the places Theresa passed on her way. Follow the stations and recall what Theresa experienced there.
Some of you might have gone similar or other ways through different places. Recall these places and tell your classmates what your experiences were.

A typical station of young Namibians in exile: The United Nations Institute for Namibia at Lusaka/Zambia.

Part IV:
Personal perspectives

Until recently, we had only one female doctor in SWAPO. But just recently another woman came from training in the Soviet Union as a medical doctor. Meanwhile, there is quite a number of us studying medicine. Some of us are soon to finish.

One thing in SWAPO is that I feel there is nothing like discrimination between the sexes. We are treated equally and can do what we want to. Coming from a background where, historically, women normally have their place in the kitchen or cannot decide what they want to do or where there is even the parents' traditional belief that as a girl you should not go to school until matriculation, I am proud to be one of the women who can now show that we are able to do such things. And nobody should stand in our way to do certain things. Whatever we want to do as long as we can manage. And I think it encourages my sisters to follow some of these examples. So that they really come up and do whatever they want to do. And that we have the right and power just like our male comrades to lead the revolution.

Now, in October 1982, at 24 years of age, I am studying medicine at the University of Zambia. It is my fourth year of studies. Altogether, I have to study for six years to become a medical doctor. Then I want to specialize as a surgeon. This will take another year. So, by early 1986 I will have finished my training.

During the holidays I do of course go back to the camps and work there. I think I will continue with such things after independence, too. Of course, then I'll be able and prepared to go back home.

For the three months holidays between the terms I go to the SWAPO camps. These holidays are from July to September, and we are a number of students, also from the United Nations Institute for Namibia. Students sometimes even come back from Europe to spend their holidays working in the SWAPO camps.

In the camps we help out in whatever field or department we receive our training. I know the situation in these camps, because it's where I come from myself. So I am used to it. And I feel I should share my education with the comrades there and not only the academic part of this education, by training nurses there. But even my general outlook about life and other things which I can share with the comrades is important. Now, since studying in Lusaka, I have made new experiences, and my own outlook has changed through contact with the local people there. And I feel that I should share these experiences with my people in the camps, who maybe sometimes think the same way I did when I was still living in the camps. So now I am going to discuss my viewpoint with them and talk about it. And maybe sometimes they change their mind as well. At the same time I am learning myself as well, and I think through contact with the people in the camps I won't have problems when I finish my studies in adjusting my mind again to the reality and minds of the people.

Of course, after our country wins independence, we will face many problems also in the health sector. For example, we will have to meet the problem of qualified persons. Especially in the rural areas, we already have to start the planning, and I feel we have to concentrate our efforts on these rural areas of Namibia. When I have finished my studies and can go back to an independent Namibia, I would like to go to one of the rural areas.

And I hope this is an idea that appeals to most of the medical students and doctors as well, because these are the areas that until now have been left out in our country. We need qualified people in the rural areas, and we should start our work there.

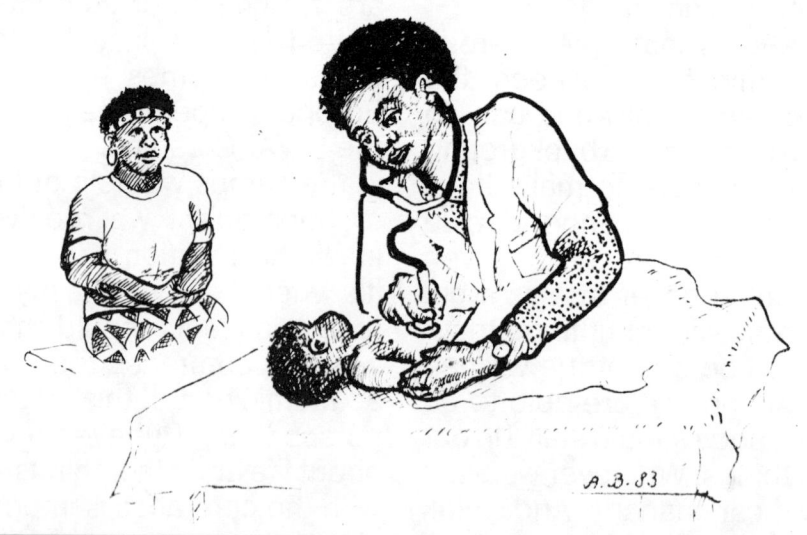

Tasks:
After reading this final section of Theresa's story, you'll notice that she is a very committed person.
— Give some examples of this commitment and discuss their meaning.
Think about your own plans in the present and future and how these are related to the independence of our country. What in your present activities do you think contributes to this independence and what do you hope to contribute in the future? Where do you see the main field of your activities and what are the reasons for your aspirations and wishes?
During the discussions in the class also consider the topic of sexual roles, as mentioned by Theresa in her story. Do you find any differences in the ambitions among boys and girls in your class? Are there any typical male or female expectations and professional aspirations that exist? If this should be the case, try to find out together what the reasons and origins of this could be.

A Visit to Kwanza Sul:

THE STRENGTH OF WOMEN

There follows an extract from a report of a visit to Kwanza Sul by a delegate of the United Nations High Commissioner for Refugees (UNHCR). It emphasises the important part of women in the daily life and the ongoing process of women taking over more responsibilities outside the household. For us, this report demonstrates the capability and dedication of the Namibian women in fulfilling the new tasks.

At the end of a valley hidden in the mountains the Kwanza Sul camp, under the blazing sun, shelters about 40.000 Namibian refugees.

Two things strike us on our arrival at Kwanza Sul: the very good morale of the refugees and the tenacity of the women. We expected to meet sad people, marked by the fact of having been uprooted for many years. But the children, the women and the old people all greet us warmly.

What is extraordinary at Kwanza Sul is the strength of the women and their participation at all levels in the camp administration: as doctors and nurses, heads of schools, sector supervisors, drivers of tanker trucks, librarians and filing clerks (yes! in Kwanza Sul they record every step in each refugee's life and each definite return to their homeland); they are all women who have studied in countries such as Tanzania, Zambia, Nigeria and the German Democratic Republic and have come back to put their knowledge at the disposal of the other Namibian refugees. Their vitality commands respect. "It is extraordinary to see the power that moves these women in such a difficult situation. There are always problems here; for example, sometimes there's no water in the camps and when there is, it's the water pumps that don't work or the tanker trucks that break down. But the women fight on against all these obstacles instead of just folding their arms and doing nothing while waiting to return to Namibia. For me it's a fantastic experience to work with them!" exclaims a Swedish doctor from his country's Solidarity Movement, who is a volunteer directing medical care at Kwanza Sul.

> **Tasks:**
> — *What do you think we should learn from these experiences?*
> — *What consequences should this have with regard to sex roles in an independent Namibia and the future of women?*

Women play an important part in all spheres of life: Students at the United Nations Institute for Namibia and women in Nyango.

Mass grave of Kassinga victims.

KASSINGA

On the 4th of May, 1978, one of SWAPO's refugee camps in southern Angola, near the town of Kassinga, was attacked and destroyed by the South African army. Kassinga had offered shelter to many Namibians who had previously left their homes. The massacre at Kassinga was one of the darkest hours in the history of our people, while at the same time once more disclosing the brutal character of the South African regime.
We should never forget the sacrifices our people had to suffer in the long and bitter history of the struggle for independence. This chapter, therefore, remembers Kassinga.

The extent of the destruction at Kassinga is described in a report by representatives from the United Nations High Commission for Refugees and the World Health Organisation, who visited the bombed camp in the same month:

"Kassinga village, which previously housed some 3000 Namibian refugees living an organized social life and having houses, schools, dispensaries, warehouses and other social installations at their disposal, for a population which was mostly composed of children, youth, women and old people, had been completely demolished. The number of victims killed by heavy bombs, fragmentation bombs, machinegun fire, as well as paralysing gas, amounts to more than 600 persons. The number wounded is more than 400. To this should be added the unknown number of dead and wounded who disappeared in the vicinity of Kassinga.

This can only be described as criminal in international law and barbaric from a moral point of view, and reminds one of the darkest episodes in modern history."

Kassinga ruins

Amelia (12 years), Julia (12 years), and Shiwonpiri (9 years) were still very young, when they tried to remember Kassinga in October 1982 at Nyango, where these eye-witnesses were then living in the Health and Education Centre. It was difficult for them to hide their emotions, when telling about the most horrifying day in their lifes so far:

"When the attack started, we were attending a general meeting. This was during the morning hours. We saw the airplanes coming, but we could not hear the engines. They came without sound.

Firstly, we did not realize that there was danger, as we could not identify the planes as South African ones. But immediately the planes started bombing, and everyone was trying to run away.

There were many people of various age at this meeting. When the bombing started, we first just stayed close to the ground. Then we started moving slowly from the open land for the river nearby to find shelter. Some bombs fell on the meeting ground, while some hit the houses. All the people were screaming and running away. A lot of them were killed on the spot. Of those who managed to escape to the nearby river, some succeeded in crossing the river, some drowned in the water. Those who managed to cross the river safely ran as fast as they could, to reach another place, where some of the people also used to stay. This was a safe place. We realized that a lot of people must have been killed. Among the dead were also some relatives of ours.

If we could, we would send back airplanes to the Boers. We still feel great sorrow and suffer from the experiences of Kassinga, where so many people have been innocently killed. We still have a great fear, even thousands of miles away from Kassinga, as soon as we hear any unfamiliar sound."

KASSINGA

Remember! And don't forget
The 4th of May 1978.
A terrible day it was.
Our people massacred in cold blood.

The enemy attacked,
She bombed and dropped.
The shells fell on civilian targets,
The buildings set ablaze.

I heard a cry of a little baby,
I heard a cry of a school going child,
I heard a cry of a pregnant woman,
A cry with pain and longing for freedom.

I saw an unbelievable scene,
It wasn't a trench but a dam.
Not of water, but of people,
A mass grave I saw with fallen Heroes.

They have died for our country,
They have died for our people.
Their blood is shed – but not in vain!
Their brightest sacrifice – won't be in vain!

The task is over to you and me,
The task is given to all of us,
We have to continue from where they ended,
Never betray their sacred blood!

Their blood is shed – but not in vain!
Their highest sacrifice – won't be in vain!
Ensure the success of the struggle!
Defend the revolution for the good of all!

Nguno Wakolele

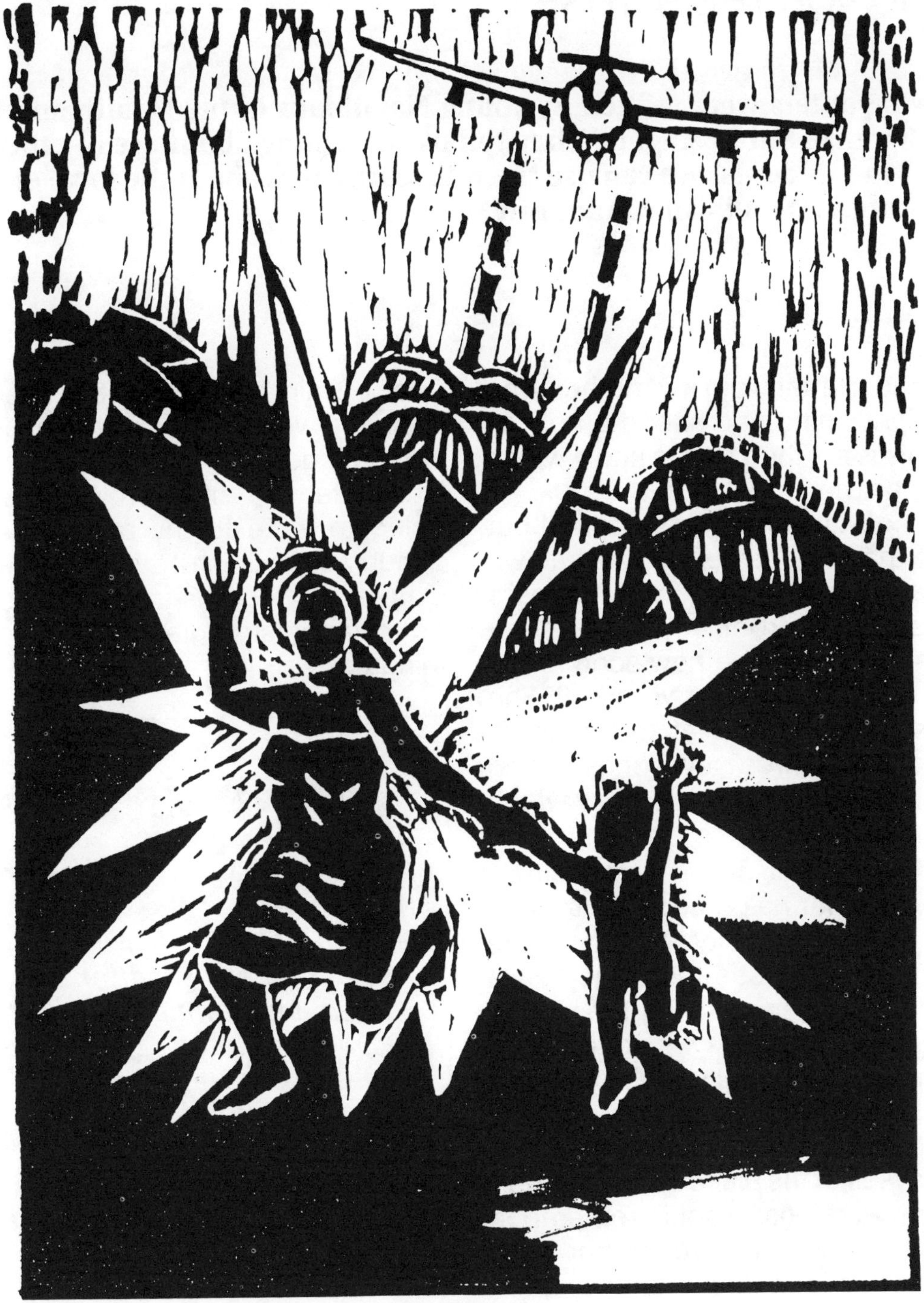

LEARNING FOR THE FUTURE

The following letters were written by young Namibians in the Health and Education Centre of Kwanza Sul in Angola. They tell us something about the life there and the activities of the students. We can use them to learn more about the local environment of this part of our Namibian community.

Dear Martha,

I have just had a letter from my mother. She said you might come and spend a holiday with us. If this is so, then let me know which day you are arriving here.

It is raining heavily here at the moment but we all hope that it stops before the time we have netball practices. The rain makes a terrific noise on the roof, while my roommate Lucia is practising a new song in the room. Therefore I can't hear very well. She said she is going to sing at the concert. She has practised three new songs during the last few days, but we don't know which one she is going to sing.

Have I told you about our history society? Our history teacher has recently started it, and I have joined the society this term. We are planning a trip to see the Cape Coast Castle. We have been studying the history of Namibian trade and now we are going to see what a castle actually looks like. I'm going to take a note-book with me, to write down the important things. So I will be able to remind myself of the place in detail, otherwise I will forget things I want to remember. We have kept rainfall records in our Geography class this term, and there has been a lot of rain, more than the average. But I hope the weather during the holidays is going to be good.

Finally, let me end here, because I'm still going to write to my parents, and I have to hurry up to finish before the netball starts. Convey my regards to all comrades I know.

Yours in the struggle,
Miriam

Tasks:
In Miriam's letter, you find some very interesting activities described, like the history-society and the rainfall-records.
— *Think about such or similar activities for investigation in your own local environment.*
— *Do you know the climate and other features around your own community?*
— *Exchange your knowledge and think about methods like those mentioned in the letter to learn more about your place.*

Miriam is trying to write a letter.

Our School

Our school's name is Namibia Education Centre. We have many teachers and students, a principal and a vice-principal in our school. There are many classes. In our Centre we also have a clinic and many nurses. In our school we have many books, pens, pencils and everything else you need and which we can use when we are in the classes. We also have a library, where we keep the books. And we have a magazine, where we keep our food. We also have kitchens of our own, where we prepare our food when we are hungry. For school we always get up early in the morning. Firstly, we go to the parade, to receive and listen to the news. Later we go to the classes. We speak English when we are in classes. Our teachers teach us how to speak and write this language.

We like our school and we go to school every day.

Amadhila

Tasks:

You are also a student in a school. Try, like Amadhila does in her letter, to give a short description of your school and its environment.

Write down what you think is important in your school and discuss the meaning and relevance of education with the others in your class.

Try to make a drawing of your school, list the number of teachers, students and classes in your school.

Our New School

In an independent Namibia, we'll have to change a lot of things in nearly all spheres of life. For too long colonialism has influenced and shaped the Namibian people and their minds. An important place for mental colonialism has everywhere been the school and the education offered to the people. Among those things to be changed, therefore, will be the education of the people. In Tanzania, for example, Education for Self-Reliance was created after independence. And another of the many examples of the re-construction of education according to the needs of the people is Mozambique.

Children at the SWAPO school on the "old farm" outside Lusaka in mid-1975 (above).
SWAPO-pioneers at a parade (below).

The following poem is taken from the diary of a teacher, later published as a book, in which he describes his experiences as a British expatriate in one of the schools in Mozambique shortly after independence. The poem has been collectively written by students of one of his classes. It expresses the spirit of the new school and mentions some of the basic changes the students and teachers together are striving for. By doing so, it offers us the chance to learn about the ideas and efforts in countries confronted with similar tasks and challenges we are facing in Namibia.
Although it is a rather lengthy poem, you should read it thoroughly.

The New School

We want to build
A new school
A true school
With conscious people
Organized and disciplined.
A new school
A true school
Where we can learn
To serve the majority -
Our community!

We want to build
A school for the People
Where everybody learns
What the People teach us -
To become at last
A school for the People.

We want to build a school
Where the People
In the person of the worker
Side by side with the peasant
Are our schoolmasters
Our guides
Our best teachers!

We want to build a school
Where the textbook is the hoe
The exercise book the pick
The pencil the good hammer -
And the rest
Spade, bucket
And screwdriver.

So our school
Won't be just four walls
But all our district
Our neighbourhood
Our community!

Today, new student
Finally
You know what to do
To study, to produce, to struggle -
Today
New student
You are servant of the People!
Defender of the country!

You always ignored
The problems of your children
And yet
You were always afraid to tread on
The white cement
Of the great schools of the minority.
You never knew them
Because they never permitted you
To enter them,
You, or your children.
The great schools of the great gentlemen
They existed
For you
Existed only
Like a vanishing wish.
You never had the hot taste of their reality
Today
Community
You are linked to the school
You live its problems directly
You and your children are prepared
Organized, orientated,
To serve the majority
You know
And live
In love of your country
With the dearness of a mother
The anxieties, the dreams, the worries
Of your children.
You

All of you
With hands clasped
Eyes to the future
Hope stamped on your faces
You make your way towards
A new Mozambique!

A school, a school for all of us
Of our parents, of all our parents
For us, with the good loud sound that calls us,
An appeal, beautiful and irresistible:
"Come and continue the task you have begun!"

Here I know who I am
Here I know where I'm going
I know here, too, for whom I'm working.

Here I breathe the Revolution
Here I live the discipline
To better know and serve my People.

Sadness and happiness I also feel
Here, on my bench with my pencil
I translate the sacrifices of my People.

Here, I feel like a bird
Young and newly born
Like a great, new school!

Today sitting at the school's desks
The school with old walls
But new heads
The eyes of the new student
Look confidently at his class.

Today
The new student
With hoe, spade, and machete,
Today
The new student
With broom and bucket
With the hose spurting out water
Today
The new student
His hands linked with his comrades'

Singing out the People's songs
Struggling against the bourgeoisie
In the school
In the neighbourhoods -
Everywhere.

Tasks:

— Summarize what is said in the previous poem by young students in Mozambique about the new school.
— Identify what seems important to you for such a new school.
— Name the differences to the experiences you had in Namibian schools under South African rule.
— Compare the aspects of the new school mentioned with what you know about SWAPO's educational principles for an independent Namibia.
— Find out how far these elements are already put into practice at the various Namibian schools (note that Namibian schools means more than schools in Namibia!).
— Discuss the above subjects in the class not only among yourselves, but also seek dialogues with the teachers to learn about their position.
— Look at the illustration on the page and tell each other what you see and read from it.
— How much do you think is it already related to yourself, your situation, your experiences, your perspectives?
— Finally, what do you think can each and every student, teacher and school-leaver contribute to the new school we have to build?
— Take the efforts of the students in Mozambique as an example and try also to write a collective poem in your class. For this, choose any subject you are interested in and is related to your school. Pin the result of your efforts to the classroom-wall.
— You could also organize a project within your school:
Each class contributes a collective poem to one or more themes relevant to your situation. You then organize a cultural meeting and read the poems to the students and teachers of the school. For this occasion, you can also invite the people living around the place of the school. You can also add drawings to the subjects dealt with in the poetry and by doing so compile a booklet from the school's students. This would be a fine document on the prevailing mood among the students and would show the sum of all your efforts to contribute your best to the new school.

Below follows another, shorter poem collectively written by students at a school in Mozambique. It deals with the activities of the students and teachers during their holidays. At the same time, it tries to meet and encounter criticism from those who have still elitist values with regard to the privileges of education and hold ignorant positions concerning the values of manual work in the country-side. These students, instead, stress the importance to be close to those people living in different spheres (locally and socially) from their own environment at school, while at the same time doing work which is as important for the country's sake as education and school is.

In the Holidays

In the holidays
Students on the road
On the way out
In the direction of the countryside
In the direction of their origin.

Students and teachers
Going to the countryside
Working, learning, and fighting
Developing their country.

Ah! The enemy's voice!
The enemy's voice cries out
Calling to his lackeys
"Look at the innocent children!
They're taking our future leaders to the countryside!
Students who already know everything
Are being taken to the countryside!"

And we students?
"Ah!" we say.
"We are children of the People
We were born in the People
We grew up in the People
And we will grow old in the People!"

Mozambican students participate in production.

Tasks:

How do you normally spend your holidays? - Try to identify the useful things you do, while at the same time don't be ashamed if you also relax in the times between what you have to do all the year round at school.

— *Discuss with each other, what purposes holidays should have and what reasons there are to spend them in one way or another. Make a list of the different possibilities and rank the various options according to your personal preferences. Then discuss the result in the classroom.*
— *Make a drawing, showing one of your favourite activities during holidays.*
— *Finally, come back to the poem about holidays. Discuss its meaning and relevance for an independent Namibia and the new school.*
— *Try to locate yourself as a student within the new Namibian society we are striving for. Where do you see your tasks and responsibilities?*

Scenes from the Namibia Health and Education Centres.

When shall I go
by Servatius Sh. Aijambo

When shall I go
To the beloved country
Where I can practice
My rights of birth?

Oh! wait dear comrade
I know when to go
Back to our country
When you'll feel at home.

But what can I do
In order to break
The chain of cruelty
of inequality and injustice?

Let me tell you
What you can do
You have no choice
But take up arms.

Take up your arms
and have no fear
Come on comrade
your gun must talk
That's your liberator.

When chains are broken
The struggle continues
That of reconstruction
of our Motherland!

APPENDIX

REFERENCES

a) Texts:
Breaking Contract. The story of Vinnia Ndadi. Recorded and edited by Dennis Mercer. Richmond/Canada: L.S.M. Information Centre 1974; pp. 20-21 (For: On contract) and p. 86 (For: Unity and self-reliance).

Robert J. Gordon,
Mines, Masters and Migrants. Life in a Namibian Mine Compound. Johannesburg: Ravan Press 1977; p. 135 (For: On colonial mentality).

Henning Melber (ed.),
It Is No More A Cry. Namibian Poetry in Exile. Basel: Basler Afrika Bibliographien 1982 (For the various poems from Namibian students).

P. Möller,
Journey in Africa through Angola, Ovampoland and Damaraland. Translated from the original Swedish edition of 1889 by Ione and Jalmar Rudner. Cape Town: C. Struik 1974; pp. 123-126 (For: From the notebook of an early European explorer).

Namibia Today. Vol. 2 No. 3, 1978; p. 15 'UN at Kassinga' (For: Kassinga).

Hinananje Shafodino Nehova,
The Price of Liberation. Published in: Liberation Support Movement (ed.), Namibia: SWAPO Fights for Freedom. Oakland/California: L.S.M. Information Centre 1978; pp. 73-78 (For: On strike).

Refugees. News from the United Nations High Commissioner for Refugees, No. 18, June 1983; 'Namibian refugees in Angola', by Djibril Diallo (For: The strength of women).

Chris Searle,
We're Building The New School! Diary of a Teacher in Mozambique. London: Zed Press 1981; p. 185 (For: Africa); pp. 35-38 and p. 172 (For: Our new school and in the holidays).

Collin O'Brien Winter
Namibia. Grand Rapids/Michigan: William B. Eerdmans Publishing Company 1977; pp. 58-59 (For: Deportation).

John Ya-Otto (with Ole Gjerstad and Michael Mercer),
Battlefront Namibia. An Autobiography. London: Heinemann 1982; pp. 49-50 (For: We won't move); p. 35 (For: The old location); p. 34 (For: The Windhoek massacre); pp. 6-7 and p. 16 (For: Life conditions of contract workers); pp. 59-61 (For: Resistance and race) and pp. 66-68 (For: Challenging the system).

b) Maps:
Felix Ermacora,
Namibia/Südwestafrika. München: Bayerische Landeszentrale für politische Bildungsarbeit 1981; p. 179 (Adopted for: Annual Rainfall) and p. 180 (Adopted for: Land Usage).

Israel Goldblatt,
History of South West Africa from the beginning of the nineteenth century. Cape Town/Wynberg/Johannesburg: Juta & Co. 1971; p. 8 (For: Settlement patterns in Namibia, around 1840).

Reginald Green/Marja-Liisa Kiljunen/Kimmo Kiljunen (eds.),
Namibia. The Last Colony. Burnt Mill/Harlow: Longman 1981; pp. 89, 92 and 95 (For: Land Distribution); p. 24 (For: Surface); p. 34 (For: Economy) and p. 36 (For: Mining). Maps drawn by Risto Kari.

Helga and Ludwig Helbig,
Mythos Deutsch-Südwest. Namibia und die Deutschen. Weinheim/Basel: Beltz 1983; p. 67 (For: The first land-theft).

Richard Moorsom,
Transforming a Wasted Land. London: The Catholic Institute for International Relations 1982; p. 13 (For: Land Use Zones).

c) Illustrations:
ccpd network letter, No. 15, July 1982; front cover (For: Africa).

Front Lines for Liberation. Poems Against Apartheid. Published by the Solidarity Committee of the German Democratic Republic; front cover (For: My mother).

Sechaba, July 1983; p. 27 (For: Kassinga).

Note:
Photos, illustrations and quotations taken from various historic sources are not in detail listed. The many photos used from the archives of the Namibia Project Group are not individually acknowledged.